Contents

ANTHROPOMETRIC STANDARDIZATION REFERENCE MANUAL

Books are to be returned on or before
the last date below.

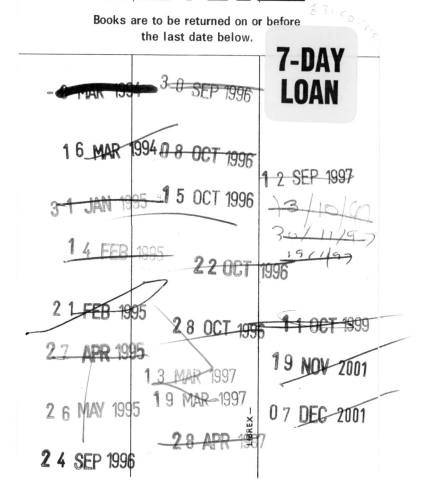

Human Kinetics Books
Champaign, Illinois

Library of Congress Cataloging-in-Publication Data

Anthropometric standardization reference manual / editors, Timothy G.
  Lohman, Alex F. Roche, Reynaldo Martorell. -- Abridged ed.
     p. cm.
     Includes bibliographical references.
     ISBN 0-87322-331-4
     1. Anthropometry. I. Lohman, Timothy G., 1940– . II. Roche,
  Alex F., 1921– . III. Martorell, Reynaldo, 1947– .
     GN51.A58   1988b
  573'.6--dc20   90-29003
                                                                                  CIP

Senior Editor: Gwen Steigelman, PhD
Production Director: Ernie Noa
Projects Manager: Lezli Harris
Managing Editor: Kari Nelson
Copy Editors: Janet Mullany and Laura E. Larson
Assistant Editor: Julie Anderson and Phaedra Hise
Proofreader: Jane Clapp
Typesetter: Theresa Bear and Kathy Boudreau-Fuoss
Text Design: Keith Blomberg
Text Layout: Denise Mueller
Cover Design: Keith Blomberg
Printed By: Braun-Brumfield

ISBN: 0-87322-331-4

Copyright © 1988, 1991 by Timothy G. Lohman, Alex F. Roche, and
Reynaldo Martorell

Printed in the United States of America

10 9 8 7 6 5 4 3 2 1

Human Kinetics Books
A Division of Human Kinetics Publishers, Inc.
Box 5076, Champaign, IL 61825-5076
1-800-747-4457

Canada Office:
Human Kinetics Publishers, Inc.
P.O. Box 2503, Windsor, ON N8Y 4S2
1-800-465-7301 (in Canada only)

UK Office:
Human Kinetics Publishers (UK) Ltd.
P.O. Box 18
Rawdon, Leeds LS19 6TG
England
(0532) 504211

781–708

Preface

This reference manual is designed to serve as a comprehensive set of measurement procedures describing over 40 anthropometric dimensions. The purpose of the manual is to provide a standardized set of descriptions that can be used across disciplines, for example, epidemiology, exercise and sport science, human biology, human nutrition, medicine, physical anthropology, and physical education.

The major impetus for developing this manual was the diverse description of measurement procedures in current use and difficulty in comparing results among investigations employing different measurement procedures. Because of the wide use of anthropometry in many fields it was considered important to develop a consensus among experts from various disciplines on a carefully developed set of procedures for future research and clinical applications of anthropometry. This project was funded by the National Institute of Child Health and Human Development; National Institutes of Arthritis, Diabetes, Digestive and Kidney Diseases; National Cancer Institute; and Ross Laboratories, Columbus, OH.

With this background a proposal was written to the National Institute of Health by Tim Lohman, who subsequently planned a concensus conference of international experts and all the steps that led to it. The conference was planned for October, 1985 in Airlie, Virginia.

Unique in the development of this reference manual is the process applied to each dimension before the final description was accepted. First, an expert was assigned by Tim Lohman to write each report giving the background literature and previous descriptions of the dimension under study. Then the expert formulated a recommended procedure for future measurements. The recommendations were sent to all members of the consensus committee who reviewed each report and rated the extent of their agreement with the pro-

posed recommendation along with suggestions for change. These critiques and ratings were summarized for each investigator and returned to the author for study and revisions. The revised reports were then sent to all participants prior to the Airlie Consensus Conference. The reports were then presented and discussed at the conference and final ratings and critiques were given by each participant. These ratings were again summarized and incorporated into final reports which were sent to Alex Roche who edited them into a common format. Photographs and illustrations were then completed at the University of Arizona and Wright State University under the supervision of Tim Lohman. Special thanks are due to Cheri Carswell and Matt Hall who were subjects for many of the photographic illustrations and for Michael Hewitt's photographic expertise.

The first edition of this reference manual also included a section on Special Issues, including right vs. left side, measurement error, and equipment availability, and a section on Applications. The papers on applications were reviewed by outside experts and edited under the supervision of Reynaldo Martorell after presentation at the Airlie Conference. These papers show the many applications of anthropometry to research involving children, the elderly, handicapped or obese individuals, clinical nutrition, epidemiology, physical anthropology, sports medicine, and coronary heart disease.

The completion of this manual was dependent on many individuals playing roles in the formulation and development of this project. The editors are extremely grateful for their contribution to this effort. Finally, we all anticipate careful use of the recommended procedures so that the efforts to produce this manual will bear greater knowledge on anthropometry and its application to many fields of study.

Airlie Conference Committee Members

Planning Conference Committee

W. Callaway, MD
G. Harrison, PhD
F. Johnston, PhD
T. Lohman, PhD

R. Martorell, PhD
A. Roche, PhD, MD
J. Wilmore, PhD

Consensus Conference Committee

R. Andres, MD
B. Bistrian, MD
G. Blackburn, PhD, MD
C. Bouchard, PhD
G. Bray, MD
E. Buskirk, PhD
C. Callaway, MD
L. Carter, PhD
C. Chumlea, PhD
W. DeWys, PhD
D. Drinkwater, PhD
P. Eveleth, PhD
R. Frisancho, PhD
C. Gordon, PhD
G. Grave, MD
S. Guo, PhD
G. Harrison, PhD
K. Hendry, PhD
S. Heymsfield, MD
J. Himes, PhD, MPH
V. Hubbard, PhD, MD
A. Jackson, PhD
C. Johnson, MSPH
F. Johnston, PhD

T. Lohman, PhD
R. Malina, PhD
A. Martin, PhD
R. Martorell, PhD
M. Micozzi, MD, PhD
C. Mitchell, PhD, RD
W. Moore, MD
W. Mueller, PhD
R. Murphy, MSPH
G. Owen, MD
M. Pollock, PhD
A. Roche, PhD, MD, DSc
W. Ross, PhD
M. Rowland, PhD
V. Seefeldt, PhD
M. Steinbaugh, PhD, RD
F. Trowbridge, PhD
T. Van Itallie, MD
J. Wilmore, PhD
C. Woteki, PhD

Introduction

People unfamiliar with anthropometry who wish to measure human beings for researcher or clinical purposes should begin by reading this manual. The advice of a trained person can be very helpful. The first steps are to select the measurements to be made, to acquire the correct instruments, and to design a recording form. The recording form should be in a format that facilitates entry of the data into a computer. The form should provide for records of the date of birth and the dates of examinations so that ages in years can be calculated to two decimal places; these calculations are best done by computer.

Practice is necessary. Reliability should be established and the best order for recording the measurements selected for a particular study should be determined. An assistant is needed to record the values read aloud by the measurer from the scales, stadiometer, caliper, or tape. More sophisticated procedures are possible by which data are automatically entered into a computer from these instruments, but these procedures are not widley used.

The measurements should be made carefully, in a quite room, without undue hast, and without the presence of unnecessary people. The measurer should note any brusing, swelling, edema, scarring, or muscle atrophy that might affect the measurements being made.

Many of the descriptions of the techniques that follow state that the subject's head should be in the Frankfort Hortizontal Plane. In this position, the most inferior point on the left orbital margin is at the same horizontal level as the left tragion. Tragion is the deepest point in the notch superior to the tragus of the auricle. When the head is in the Frankfort Horizontal Plane the line of vision (''look straight ahead'') is approximately horzontal, and the sagittal plane of the head is vertical.

Full reference citations are located at the end of chapter 5. However, abbreviated references (author and date) relevant to each topic are provided throughout each of the chapters for the reader's convenience. Also four compendiums, listed among the literature cited, may be useful as source books for other tenchiques and sets of reference data. These are the publications of Garrett and Kennedy, 1971; *Anthropometric Source Book* (National Aeronautics and Space Administration, 1978); Malina and Roche, 1983; and Roche and Malina 1983.

Chapter 1

Stature, Recumbent Length, and Weight

Claire C. Gordon,
William Cameron Chumlea, and
Alex F. Roche

Stature

Recommended Technique

The measurement of stature requires a vertical board with an attached metric rule and a horizontal headboard that can be brought into contact with the most superior point on the head (see Figure 1). The combination of these elements is called a "stadiometer." Fixed and portable models are available, and plans to assist fabrication of a stadi-

ometer by an investigator are available from the Field Services Branch, Division of Nutrition, Centers for Disease Control, Atlanta, Georgia 30333.

The subject is barefoot or wears thin socks and wears little clothing so that the positioning of the body can be seen. The subject stands on a flat surface that is at a right angle to the vertical board of the stadiometer (see Figure 2). The weight of the subject is distributed evenly on both feet, and the head is positioned in the Frankfort Horizontal Plane. The arms hang freely by the sides of the

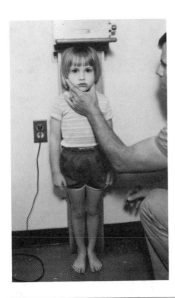

Figure 1 Measurement of stature using stadiometer (front view).

Figure 2 Measurement of stature using stadiometer (side view).

trunk, with the palms facing the thighs. The subject places the heels together, with both heels touching the base of the vertical board. The medial borders of the feet are at an angle of about 60°. If the subject has knock knees, the feet are separated so that the medial borders of the knees are in contact but not overlapping. The scapulae and buttocks are in contact with the vertical board. The heels, buttocks, scapulae, and the posterior aspect of the cranium of some subjects cannot be placed in one vertical plane while maintaining a reasonable natural stance. These subjects are positioned so that only the buttocks and the heels or the cranium are in contact with the vertical board.

The subject is asked to inhale deeply and maintain a fully erect position without altering the load on the heels. The movable headboard is brought onto the most superior point on the head with sufficient pressure to compress the hair. The measurement is recorded to the nearest 0.1 cm, and the time at which the measurement was made is noted.

Recumbent length is measured in place of stature until the age of two years. Between 2 and 3 years, recumbent length or stature can be measured, and the choice made between these variables must be noted because they differ systematically. Two measurers are needed to measure stature in children aged 2 to 3 years. One measurer places a hand on the child's feet to prevent lifting of the heels and to keep the heels against the vertical board and makes sure the knees are extended with the other hand. The second measurer lowers the headboard and observes its level.

When there is lower limb anisomelia (inequality of length), the shorter side is built up with graduated wooden boards until the pelvis is level, as judged from the iliac crests. The amount of the buildup is recorded because it can alter the interpretation of weight-stature relationships.

Purpose

Stature is a major indicator of general body size and of bone length. It is important in screening for disease or malnutrition and in the interpretation of weight. Variations from the normal range can have social consequences, in addition to their associations with disease.

When stature cannot be measured, recumbent length can be substituted and, depending on the purpose of the study, adjustments for the systematic differences between these highly correlated

measurements may be desirable (Roche & Davila, 1974). Arm span may be used in place of stature, when stature cannot be measured and it is not practical to measure recumbent length. The measurement of arm span is described in the section on segment lengths. Also, stature can be estimated from knee height as described in the section on recumbent anthropometry.

Literature

Stature can be measured using a fixed or movable anthropometer. An anthropometer consists of a vertical graduated rod and a movable rod that is brought onto the head. An anthropometer can be attached to a wall or used in a free-standing mode using a base plate to keep the vertical rod properly aligned (see Figures 3, 4, and 5; Hertzberg et al., 1963). Measurements of stature with a movable

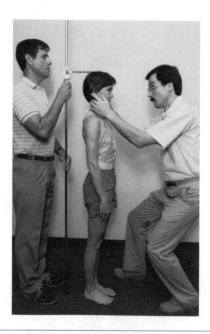

Figure 3 Measurement of stature using moveable anthropometer (side view).

anthropometer tend to be less than those with a stadiometer (Damon, 1964). It is not recommended that stature be measured against a wall, but if this must be done, a wall should be chosen that does not have a baseboard, and the subject should not stand on a carpet. An apparatus that allows stature to be measured while the subject stands on a platform scale is not recommended.

Some workers have not asked subjects to stretch to an unusual extent. This is likely to lead to less reproducible positioning and less reliability than

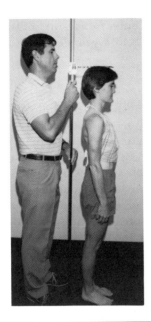

Figure 4 Measurement of stature using moveable anthropometer (side view).

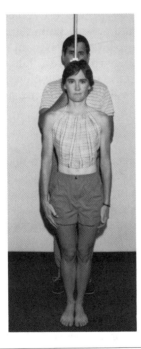

Figure 5 Measurement of stature using moveable anthropometer (front view).

the recommended procedure. Some workers ask the subjects to assume a position of military attention; this is inappropriate for young children and for the elderly. In one alternative technique, a measurer exerts upward force under the mastoid processes to keep the head at the maximum level to which it was raised when the subject inhaled

deeply. A second measurer lowers the headboard and observes its level, while a third person records the value (Weiner & Lourie, 1981). The need for three measurers reduces the practicality of this technique, but when it is applied the diurnal variation in stature is reduced (Whitehouse et al., 1974).

Some workers place the head in a "normal" position, with the eyes looking straight ahead; this is less precise than positioning in the Frankfort Horizontal Plane. Others tilt the head backwards and forwards and record stature when the head is positioned so that the maximum value is obtained. It is difficult to apply the latter procedure while the subject maintains a full inspiration.

It is general practice to place the subject's heels together but the angle between the medial borders has varied from study to study. If these borders are parallel, or nearly so, many young children and some obese adults are unable to stand erect.

Reliability

Intermeasurer differences for large samples in the Fels Longitudinal Study are as follows: $M = 2.4$ mm $(SD = 2.1$ mm$)$ at 5 to 10 years; $M = 2.0$ mm $(SD = 1.9$ mm$)$ at 10 to 15 years; $M = 2.3$ mm $(SD = 2.4$ mm$)$ at 15 to 20 years; $M = 1.4$ mm $(SD = 1.5$ mm$)$ at 20 to 55 years, and $M = 2.1$ mm $(SD = 2.1$ mm$)$ at 54 to 85 years (Chumlea & Roche, 1979).

Sources of Reference Data

Children
Demirjian, 1980
Demirjian et al., 1972
Hamill et al., 1977, 1979
Kondo & Eto, 1975
Wilson, 1979

Adults
Abraham et al., 1979
National Aeronautics and Space Administration, 1978

Recumbent Length

Recommended Technique

Two observers are required to measure recumbent length. The subject lies in a supine position upon a recumbent length table (see Figure 6). The crown of the head touches the stationary, vertical headboard, and the center line of the body coincides with the center line of the measuring table. The

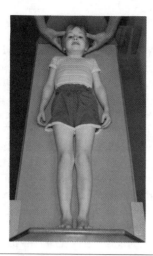

Figure 6   Subject in supine position for recumbent length.

subject's head is held with the Frankfort Plane aligned perpendicular to the plane of the measuring table. The shoulders and buttocks are flat against the tabletop, with the shoulders and hips aligned at right angles to the long axis of the body. The legs are extended at the hips and knees and lie flat against the tabletop, with the arms resting against the sides of the trunk. The measurer positioning the head stands behind the end of the table to ensure that the subject does not change position and to check the alignment of the body with the long axis of the table. The second measurer places one hand on the knees to ensure that the legs remain flat on the table. He or she applies firm pressure with the other hand to shift the movable board against the heels (see Figure 7). The length is recorded to the nearest 0.1 cm.

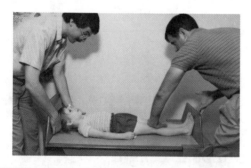

Figure 7   Measurement of recumbent length.

Purpose

Recumbent length is usually measured in those who are unable to stand erect or for whom stature would be spurious. It is an important measure of total skeletal length in infants and small children. Recumbent length is required for comparison with the National Center for Health Statistics reference data from birth to 3 years.

Literature

Recumbent length is measured commonly in infants but not at older ages. As a result, it is frequently omitted from texts on anthropometry (Olivier, 1969). Recumbent length should be measured on a table that has a fixed headboard and a movable footboard that are each perpendicular to the suface of the table. A measuring tape is needed along one or both sides of the table, with the zero end at the junction of the headboard and table surface (Moore & Roche, 1983).

There are only small differences among reported techniques of measurement (Cameron, 1984; Moore & Roche, 1983; Snyder et al., 1975; Snyder et al., 1977; Weiner & Lourie, 1981). For the accurate measurement of recumbent length, the head must be in firm contact with the headboard, the body positioned straight along the table, and the legs extended with the soles vertical. For an uncooperative child or very young infant, it may be necessary to apply gentle restraint to ensure adequate positioning. The more a child or infant deviates from the standard positioning, the poorer the reliability and validity of the measurement.

Reliability

Reliability for recumbent length should be good. Nevertheless, because recumbent length is commonly measured in infants and small children, some of whom are uncooperative, reliability is less than that for stature at older ages. Measurer variability is affected by the amount of pressure applied to the sliding footboard. Pressure should be sufficient to compress the soft tissues of the foot but not enough to alter the length of the vertebral column (Cameron, 1984). In the Fels Longitudinal Study, the mean absolute intermeasurer error for children, birth to 6 years of age, was 0.28 cm (Chumlea & Roche, 1979).

Sources of Reference Data

Children
Roche & Malina, 1983
Snyder et al., 1975, 1977

Adults
Roche & Malina, 1983
Hamill et al., 1977, 1979
Snyder et al., 1977

Weight

Recommended Technique

During infancy, a leveled pan scale with a beam and movable weights is used. The pan must be at least 100 cm long so that it can support a 2-year-old infant at the 95th percentile for recumbent length. A quilt is left on the scale at all times and the scale calibrated to zero and across the range of expected weights, when only a quilt is on it, using test objects of known weights. Calibration is performed monthly and whenever the scales are moved. Similar procedures are used to calibrate the scales used for older individuals. When the scales are not in use, the beam should be locked in place or the weights shifted from zero to reduce wear.

The infant, with or without a diaper, is placed on the scales so that the weight is distributed equally on each side of the center of the pan (see Figure 8). Weight is recorded, to the nearest 10 g,

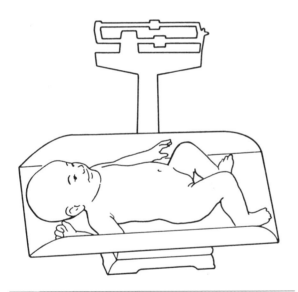

Figure 8 Infant positioned on a pan scale for the measurement of weight.

with the infant lying quietly, which may require patience. When an infant is restless, it is possible to weigh the mother when holding the infant and then weigh the mother without the infant, but this procedure is unreliable, partly because the mother's weight will be recorded to the nearest 100 g. It is better to postpone the measurement and try later. The measurement is repeated three times and the average recorded after excluding any clearly erroneous value. If a diaper is worn, the weight of the diaper is subtracted from the ob-

served weight because most reference data for infants are based on nude weights.

In a clinic, the measured weight is recorded in tabular form, in addition to being plotted. This plotting is done while the subject is present. Irregularities may be noted in the serial data for a subject or there may be major discrepancies between the percentile levels for highly correlated variables. When this occurs, the measurer checks the accuracy of the plotting and remeasures the subject if the plotting is correct.

A subject able to stand without support is weighed using a leveled platform scale with a beam and moveable weights (Figure 9). The beam

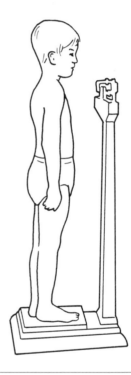

Figure 9 Subject positioned on a leveled platform scale for the measurement of weight.

on the scale must be graduated so that it can be read from both sides and the scale positioned so that the measurer can stand behind the beam, facing the subject, and can move the beam weights without reaching around the subject. The movable tare is arranged so that a screwdriver is needed to shift it. The subject stands still over the center of the platform with the body weight evenly distributed between both feet. Light indoor clothing can be worn, excluding shoes, long trousers, and sweater. It is better to standardize the clothing, for example, a disposable paper gown. The weight of this clothing is not subtracted from the observed weight when the recommended reference data are used. Weight is recorded to he nearest 100 g.

Handicapped subjects, other than infants, who cannot stand unsupported can be weighed using a beam chair scale or bed scale. If an adult weighs more than the upper limit on the beam, a weight can be suspended from the left-hand end of the beam after which the measurer must determine how much weight must be placed on the platform for the scale to record zero when there is no weight on the platform. This weight is added to the measured value when a scale modified in this fashion is used. In studies to assess short-term changes, weights must be recorded at times standardized in relation to ingestion, micturition, and defecation; generally this is not necessary.

Purpose

Weight is the most commonly recorded anthropometric variable, and generally it is measured with sufficient accuracy. Accuracy can be improved, however, by attention to details of the measurement technique. Strictly, this measurement is of mass rather than weight, but the latter term is too well established to be replaced easily. Weight is a composite measure of total body size. It is important in screening for unusual growth, obesity, and undernutrition.

Literature

There is general agreement that weight should be measured using a beam scale with movable weights and that a pan scale is needed for measurements made during infancy. The use of a spring scale is not recommended, despite its greater mobility, except in field conditions where there may be no practical alternative. Accurate electronic scales are available that are lighter than beam scales. These are expected to replace beam scales. Automatic scales that print the weight directly onto a permanent record are available but expensive. The scale should be placed with the platform level and in a position where the measurer can see the back of the beam without leaning around the subject. Scales with wheels to facilitate movement from one location to another are not recommended, because they need calibration every time they are moved.

Weight is best measured with the subject nude, which is practical during infancy (Moore & Roche, 1983). At older ages, nude measurements may not be possible (Tuddenham & Snyder, 1954). If not, standardized light clothing, for example, a disposable paper gown, should be worn (Hamill et al., 1970) in preference to "light indoor clothing" (Van Wieringen et al., 1971).

There are diurnal variations in weight of about 1 kg in children and 2 kg in adults. Therefore, recording the time of day at which measurements are made is necessary (Krogman, 1950; Sumner & Whitacre, 1931). Usually it is not practical to measure at a fixed time, but a narrow range may be achievable.

Reliability

Intermeasurer differences in the Fels Longitudinal Study are as follows: $M = 1.2$ g ($SD = 3.2$ g) at 5 to 10 years; $M = 1.5$ g ($SD = 3.6$ g) at 10 to 15 years; 1.7 g ($SD = 3.8$ g) at 15 to 20 years; and $M = 1.5$ g ($SD = 3.6$ g) for adults (Chumlea & Roche, 1979). In the Health Examination Survey by the National Center for Health Statistics, the intermeasurer and intrameasurer technical errors were about 1.2 kg, when pairs of measurements were made 2 weeks apart (Hamill et al., 1973a). About 10% of the observed error would have been due to growth.

Sources of Reference Data

Children
Hamill et al., 1977, 1979

Adults
Abraham et al., 1979

Chapter 2

Segment Lengths

Alan D. Martin,
J.E. Lindsay Carter,
Keith C. Hendy, and
Robert M. Malina

Lengths of Segments

Purpose

Stature is a composite measurement, including the lower extremities, trunk, neck, and head. Thus, stature can be viewed as comprising several segments. The same is true of the total lower and upper extremity lengths, that is, each consists of several segments. In addition to providing information on the differential contribution of specific segments to overall body size and to understanding differential growth and human variation in size and proportions, segment lengths are of clinical and occupational utility. In the former, many syndromes that involve dysmorphology are characterized by disproportionate limb or segment-length growth. As such, specific segment lengths, and more important, the ratios between segment lengths, are of diagnostic utility in studies of dysmorphology (Robinow & Chumlea, 1982; Smith, 1976). In the occupational context—for example, work space and equipment design, clothing and furniture manufacture, and safe toy design—information on specific segment lengths and other anthropometric dimensions are central. Applied anthropometry, also labeled human factors or ergonomics, uses a more comprehensive set of anthropometric dimensions, including both static and functional (dynamic) measurements, that are beyond the scope of this manual (Damon et al., 1966; Garrett & Kennedy, 1971; Hertzberg et al., 1963; Malina et al., 1973; Martin, 1954; Roche & Malina, 1983; Snyder et al., 1977).

This statement considers several aspects of the measurement and application of segment lengths. Details of the techniques of measurement of selected segments are given in subsequent sections.

Segment lengths are most commonly measured between specific bony landmarks and as vertical distances between a flat surface and a bony landmark. They should not be measured from joint creases.

Projected Versus Direct Measurements

Segments can be measured as heights or lengths. The former are vertical distances from the surface upon which the subject stands or sits to the particular landmark. The difference between the heights of two landmarks gives an estimate of a segment length. For example, acromiale height minus radiale height gives an estimate of upper arm length (acromiale is the most superior point on the lateral border of the acromial process; radiale is the most proximal point on the head of the radius); or, standing height minus suprasternale height gives an estimate of the height of the "neck plus head" (suprasternale is the most superior point on the manubrium in the midline). Lengths can be measured in the long axis of the segment as the distances between specific landmarks. As a rule, segment lengths measured directly between landmarks are greater than those derived as the differences between pairs of heights.

Estimates of segment lengths from specific pairs of heights are called *projected measurements*. Height measurements are perpendicular distances between pairs of landmarks, although the specific bone represented by the bony landmarks commonly has a slightly oblique orientation (Wilder, 1920).

Other problems with projected measurements relate to subject positioning and measurement errors. Most subjects have difficulty holding the standard erect posture (see the following section) for the time necessary to take a series of height measurements. This is particularly true in children and the elderly. And because two measurements are involved in deriving any projected segment length, there are two sources of measurement variability.

Subject Positioning

Most segment-length measurements are made with the subject standing in a position called *the standard erect posture,* that is, erect with the heels together and the upper limbs hanging at the sides. There is some variation in head position, some calling for the Frankfort Horizontal Plane (Cameron, 1978; Krogman, 1950), others calling for the head erect, looking straight ahead, so that the visual axis is parallel to the surface of the floor (Hrdlička, 1939; Montagu, 1960), or the head poised so that the visual axis is horizontal. The latter two descriptions essentially approximate the Frankfort Plane. Some describe the standard erect position as the "military position" (Montagu, 1960; Wilder, 1920), which generally implies the position of attention, with the shoulders drawn back, the chest projected forward, and the palms facing anteriorly. Positioning of the upper extremities is important in the measurement of segment lengths. In the standard position, the upper extremities are pendant at the sides, with the palms facing medially.

Some segment lengths are measured with the subject in the seated position, for example, sitting height. The subject sits erect with the head in the Frankfort Horizontal Plane and the thighs horizontal. In most directives, the legs hang freely over the edge of the sitting surface, although some special measuring tables have a built-in adjustable foot rest (see Sitting Height section for specific details).

Issues and Suggestions

Obviously, the measurements selected depend on the purpose of the study; that is, each measurement is designed to provide specific information within the context of the study. Hence, no single battery of segment measurements will meet the needs of every study. Where possible, directly

measured segment lengths are preferred over projected lengths.

Although landmarks are specifically defined anatomically, some are difficult to locate. Some of the landmarks are not ossified at young ages; they are present in cartilage but are difficult to palpate. Hence, radiographic methods may be more appropriate to study extremity segment lengths in children younger than 10 years, but there are limitations to radiography that include irradiation, correction for distortion and magnification, consistent positioning, and cost.

Upper Extremity.   Measurement of upper extremity segment lengths should be made directly from landmark to landmark, with the subject in the standard erect position:

- Total length—acromiale to dactylion.
- Upper arm—acromiale to the olecranon.
- Forearm—radiale to stylion.
- Total arm—acromiale to stylion.
- Hand—stylion to dactylion.

Dactylion is the most distal point on the middle finger, excluding the nail; *stylion* is the most distal point on the lateral margin of the styloid process of the radius.

Valk (1971, 1972) has described an apparatus to measure ulnar length, which permits the study of segment growth during intervals of 1 to 3 weeks. This is of clinical relevance in situations where it may be essential to monitor short-term growth, as during hormonal therapy. The forearm and hand are fixed in the apparatus, and the measurement is made from the olecranon to the "dividing line" between the triquetral and the ulnar styloid process.

Lower Extremity.   The measurement of the length of the lower extremity and its specific segments is not as straightforward as for the upper extremity. Thigh length is measured from the inguinal ligament to the patella. Calf length is measured directly from tibiale to sphyrion, with the subject seated and the ankle resting on the opposite knee (Cameron, 1978). *(Tibiale* is the most superior point on the medial border of the medial condyle of the tibia; *sphyrion* is the most inferior point on the medial malleolus.) Foot length is measured directly as the maximum distance from the most posterior point on the heel *(acropodion)* to the tip of the most anteriorly projecting toe *(pternion;* Montagu, 1960; Wilder, 1920). Foot length can be measured with weight bearing (Montagu, 1960; Olivier, 1969;

Wilder, 1920) or without weight bearing (Cameron, 1978).

Stature minus sitting height is often used to provide an estimate of lower extremity *(subischial)* height. Other estimates of lower extremity length are symphysion, iliospinale, and trochanterion heights. *Symphysion* is the most superior point on the pubic arch in the midline, *iliospinale* is the most anterior point on the anterior superior iliac spine, and *trochanterion* is the most superior point on the greater trochanter. These three landmarks are difficult to locate, and none aligns with the head of the femur. The average of symphyseal height and iliospinal height is occasionally used to define inguinale, ''which (corroborated by dissection) is at, or a bit above, the top of the femoral head'' (Krogman, 1970, p. 9). Thigh length is ordinarily projected as the difference between iliospinale and tibiale heights, although it has been projected as the difference between inguinale and tibiale height (Krogman, 1970).

Valk et al. (1983a, 1983b) have described an apparatus for the measurement of lower leg length, which, as in the case for the apparatus for ulnar length, is designed to permit the study of segment growth during short intervals. Lower leg length is measured as the greatest distance between the measurement surface and the footstool. The measurement requires an adjustable chair that positions the thigh and calf of the subject at an angle less than 90° and permits medio lateral and antero posterior movements of the leg. The former is necessary so that the measurement surface touches the knee instead of the upper leg, whereas the latter permits movement of the leg to obtain the greatest distance.

Sitting height is a composite of trunk, neck, and head heights (see Sitting Height). It is often used as a measure of the length of the upper segment of the body. Specific segments of sitting height can be estimated. *Cervicale height sitting* and *suprasternale height sitting* are occasionally used to estimate trunk length excluding the neck and head, whereas *tragion height sitting* is used to estimate trunk length including the neck (Wilder, 1920). *(Tragion* is the deepest point in the notch just superior to the tragus of the auricle.) Sitting height minus *suprasternale height sitting* is used to estimate the height of the head plus neck (Montagu, 1960). In the standing position, the difference between suprasternale and symphysion heights is occasionally used to project anterior trunk length (Krogman, 1970; Olivier, 1969).

Some literature indicates the clinical utility of up-

per and lower segment heights, in contrast to sitting height (Engelbach, 1932; Smith, 1976). Symphyseal height is the usual clinical measure of lower segment height, whereas stature minus symphyseal height is the usual clinical measure of upper segment height. The two heights are ordinarily used to obtain a ratio.

Difficulties in measuring symphyseal height have been indicated earlier. Engelbach (1932) recommends that both upper and lower segment lengths be measured directly with the subject supine.

Although not a segment length per se, arm span is another composite measurement that includes both upper extremities and the breadth across the shoulders. It may have clinical relevance in cases in which stature or recumbent length cannot be measured (see Arm Span section later in this chapter).

Many segment lengths are used in the form of ratios, the most common being the ratio of sitting height to stature. As with specific segment lengths, the ratio of choice depends on the problem under study.

Sitting Height

Recommended Technique

The measurement of sitting height requires a table, an anthropometer, and a base for the anthropometer. The table should be sufficiently high so that the subject's legs hang freely. The subject sits on the table with the legs hanging unsupported over the edge of the table and with the hands resting on the thighs in a cross-handed position (see Figure 1). The knees are directed straight ahead. The backs of the knees are near the edge of the table but not in contact with it. The subject sits as erect as possible, with the head in the Frankfort Horizontal Plane. In positioning, it is useful to approach the subject from the left side and to apply gentle pressure simultaneously with the right hand over the lumbar area and with the left hand on the superior part of the sternum. This reinforces the erect position. Gentle upward traction on the mastoid processes ensures the fully erect seated posture.

The lower half of the anthropometer is set in its base, and it is positioned vertically in the midline behind the subject so that it nearly touches the sacral and interscapular regions. When almost ready to make the measurement, the measurer ap-

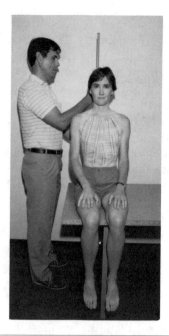

Figure 1   Measurement of sitting height (front view).

proaches from the subject's left side. The measurer's left hand is placed under the subject's chin to assist in holding the proper position, and the right hand moves the blade of the anthropometer onto the vertex (the most superior point on the head in the sagittal plane (see Figure 2). When the subject and measurer are so positioned, the subject is instructed to take a deep breath, and the measurement is made just before the subject

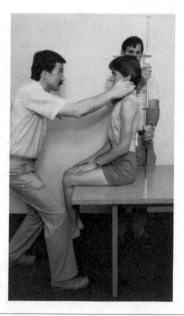

Figure 2   Side view of sitting height measurement illustrating proper positioning of subject.

exhales. Firm pressure is applied to compress the hair. The measurer should observe the level of the anthropometer blade without parallax; hence, a small stool may be required. The measurement is recorded to the nearest 0.1 cm.

It is important that the recorder observe both the position of the subject to avoid slouching and also the position of the anthropometer to ensure that it is vertical and that the blade is brought down in the midline of the head. If too much pressure is applied to the anthropometer blade, it may slide to one side off the vertex. It is important that the subject's arms rest relaxed on the thighs. The subjects should not place their hands on the side of the table and push themselves erect. This procedure may elevate the subjects, ever so slightly, off the table surface.

Purpose

Sitting height is a measure of the distance from the seating surface to the vertex. It is a composite measurement that includes the trunk, neck, and head. When the subject is seated, the body weight is supported by the ischia, therefore, the lower extremities contribute little to the measurement. Thus, "stature minus sitting height" provides an estimate of lower extremity or subischial height (see general statement on segment lengths). Sitting height should not be measured with the subject sitting on the floor or other flat surface with the legs extended. Crown-rump length (discussed in more detail in the following section) corresponds to sitting height and is measured in the first 2 to 3 years of life.

The ratio of sitting height to stature (Cormic Index), or crown-rump length to recumbent length in the first 2 to 3 years of life, is highest in infancy and decreases during childhood. Generally the lower value occurs early in pubescence due to the early growth of the lower extremities relative to the trunk. The ratio also shows ethnic/racial variation. It tends to be lowest in black populations, intermediate in white populations, and highest in Asiatic populations.

Literature

Sitting height can be measured with special equipment or with a modification of the procedures used for measuring stature. A special sitting-height measuring table is available (Cameron, 1978) that is equipped with an adjustable footrest so that the subject's legs do not hang unsupported and with a movable back piece that is moved toward the subject's buttocks. The back piece has a movable, horizontal headboard that can be brought in contact with the subject's head. Subject positioning is the same as in the recommended technique, except that the legs are supported by the footrest so that the thighs are horizontal. The use of the special measuring table or the recommended technique gives results that are in close agreement, but the latter is used more commonly.

The technique applied at the Fels Research Institute (Hrdlička, 1939; Roche & Chumlea, personal communication, 1985) uses a rectangular box (50 × 40 × 30 cm) as the sitting surface. The box is placed in front of a stadiometer. Subject position is as described above, except that the legs may or may not hang unsupported depending on the size of the subject. The subject is seated so that the buttocks are in contact with the backboard of the stadiometer. Depending on the size of the subject, the box may have to be rotated so that the subject's buttocks are in contact with the backboard. When the subject is seated properly, the headboard of the stadiometer is brought down onto the head as in the measurement of stature, and the reading is taken. Subsequently, 50 cm (the height of the box or sitting surface) is subtracted from the recorded reading to estimate sitting height. The box should not be so low that the thighs are not horizontal (Hrdlička, 1939).

Sitting height in the supine position has also been reported. A special table is used so that the measurement procedures are identical with those for sitting height in the erect position (Snyder et al., 1977). As expected, the supine measurement is longer than the seated measurement, but it closely approximates crown-rump length.

Reliability

The technical errors of measurement for sitting height in the U.S. Health Examination Survey of youth 12 through 17 years of age were 0.5 (intrameasurer) and 0.7 cm (intermeasurer), whereas the median intra- and intermeasurer differences were 0.4 cm and 0.7 cm, respectively (Malina et al., 1974). Intrameasurer technical errors of measurement for five studies of school-aged children from several ethnic groups at the University of Texas at Austin ranged between 0.1 cm and 0.7 cm, whereas the intermeasurer technical error of measurement in one study was 0.4 cm (Malina, 1986). Larger technical errors of measurement occurred in studies in which the replicate measurements were done about 1 month apart (0.6 and 0.7 cm), the smaller error estimates occurred in studies

in which the replicates were done the same day (0.1 to 0.3 cm).

Sources of Reference Data

Children

Hamill et al., 1973b
Johnson et al., 1981
Kondo & Eto, 1975
Malina et al., 1974
Snyder et al., 1977

Adults

Johnson et al., 1981

Crown-Rump Length

Recommended Technique

Two observers are required to measure crown-rump length. The subject lies in a supine position upon a recumbent-length board. The crown of the head touches the stationary, vertical headboard, with the long axis of the body coinciding with the long axis of the board. The subject's head is held with the Frankfort Plane perpendicular to the plane of the board (see Figure 3). The shoulders

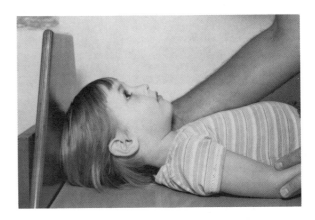

Figure 3 Positioning of head for crown-rump length.

and hips should be flat against the board and aligned at right angles to the long axis of the body (see Figure 4). The observer positioning the head stands behind the end of the board to ensure that the long axis of the subject coincides with the long axis of the board. The second observer raises the legs so that the thighs are at an angle of 90° to the surface of the board and, with the other hand, moves the sliding board against the buttocks with

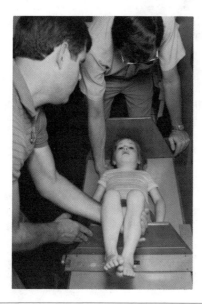

Figure 4 Positioning of truck and legs for crown-rump length.

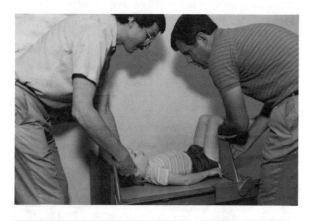

Figure 5 Measurement of crown-rump length.

firm pressure (see Figure 5). The measurement is recorded to the nearest 0.1 cm.

Purpose

Crown-rump length corresponds to sitting height in older children and adults. It is a measure of trunk length. It must be measured in place of sitting height when a measurement of trunk length is required and when the subject is unable to sit with the positioning recommended for sitting height.

Literature

The recommended methodology corresponds to that used in many studies (Cameron, 1984; Moore

& Roche, 1983; Snyder et al., 1975, 1977). The equipment needed is the same as for recumbent length, but during infancy, when the measurement is most common, a recumbent-length board can be used in place of a recumbent-length table.

Reliability

This measurement is slightly more reliable than sitting height at corresponding ages, but the differences are small. In the Fels Longitudinal Study, the mean absolute intermeasurer error for 40 boys and 25 girls, birth to 6 years of age, was 0.18 cm (Chumlea & Roche, 1979). In the Oakland Growth Study, the mean absolute intermeasurer error for stem length in adolescent boys was 1.3 cm (Stolz & Stolz, 1951). Stem length is closely similar to crown-rump length.

Sources of Reference Data

Children
McCammon, 1970
Snyder et al., 1975, 1977

Adults
None reported

Lower Extremity Length (Subischial Height)

Recommended Technique

Lower extremity length is the distance between the hip joint and the floor when the subject stands erect. In the living it can only be approximated because of the difficulty of precisely locating the hip joint. Functionally it is often defined as the difference between stature and sitting height. In those unable to stand or sit in the recommended manner, the difference between recumbent length and crown-rump length is used. These are the recommended measures; the techniques for determining them are described elsewhere.

Purpose

Lower extremity length is useful in studies of proportion, performance, and human engineering.

Literature

Literature is described under the separate measurements (stature, recumbent length, sitting height, crown-rump length).

Differences in landmark location among studies relate mainly to the proximal terminus. The *distal site* is defined as the floor (stature) or the soles of the feet (recumbent length). If sitting height or crown-rump length is used, lower extremity length is the distance between the inferior aspect of the ischial tuberosity and any compressed soft tissues to the distal landmark. Clearly this is an underestimate of the true length and is more correctly called subischial height.

The possible alternatives to sitting height are discussed in the Sitting Height section. Martin and Saller (1959) provide corrections that can be applied to some of these projected heights to estimate the center of the hip joint, but these corrections are sample specific. The landmarks that best approximate the level of the hip joint are symphysion (De Garay et al., 1974), gluteal arch, or trochanteric height (Ross et al., 1978), providing the pelvis is not tilted too far forward or backward, but it is difficult to identify these landmarks in all subjects (see Figure 6).

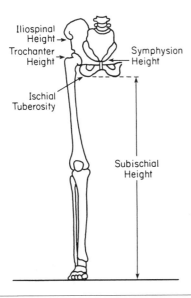

Figure 6   Illustration of subischial height.

The choice of measures depends on the objective. When stature and sitting height have been measured, lower extremity length is not always analyzed as a separate "measure" because it does not provide independent information.

Reliability

This is described in the statements for the separate measures.

Sources of Reference Data

Children

Roche & Malina, 1983
Zavaleta, 1976

Adults

Churchill et al., 1977
Clauser et al., 1972
McConville et al., 1977

Thigh Length

Recommended Technique

Thigh length is defined anatomically as hip-knee length; its measurement in the living is approximate because it is difficult to locate these joints. In the living, its measurement is either "direct" or "projected." Direct thigh length is measured from the midpoint of the inguinal ligament to the proximal edge of the patella (see Figure 7). The location of these points is described in the section on thigh skinfold. A nonstretchable tape measure is used. Projected thigh length is the difference between sitting height and tibial height. To obtain projected thigh length, the recommended technique for measuring sitting height is applied and tibial height is measured also. A table or special chair and an anthropometer are needed. The more desirable measure is direct thigh length.

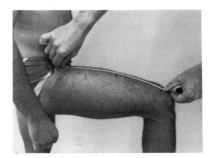

Figure 7   Measurement of direct thigh length.

Purpose

Thigh length is useful in studies of body proportions and in human engineering.

Literature

The literature relating to the proximal landmark is covered under thigh skinfold; the distal point is covered under calf length.

Sitting height is recommended as the proximal reference for the indirect measurement because of its common inclusion in anthropometric surveys (Clauser et al., 1972; Eveleth & Tanner, 1976; Hertzberg et al., 1963). Projected thigh length can be obtained also by subtracting tibiale height from symphysial, crotch, iliospinal, trochanteric, buttock, gluteal furrow, or gluteal arch height. These procedures are not recommened, partly because the set of recorded measurements would be increased. The symphysial and crotch landmarks will not be accepted by many subjects. The iliospinal and gluteal furrow levels do not provide good approximations to the location of the hip joint, and the trochanteric, buttock, and gluteal arch points cannot be located reliably. Buttock-knee or buttock-popliteal length are other indices of thigh length (Clauser et al., 1972; Weiner & Lourie, 1981). Crown-rump length is substituted for sitting height in those unable to sit in the recommended position (Cameron, 1984).

The choice of measures depends, in part, on the objectives. If lower extremity segments are to be summed, it is best to select a thigh-length measure that will not overlap with other segment lengths. This also serves as an error check if the sum of the segments is matched with another measure. For example, stature is equivalent to sitting height plus thigh length plus tibiale height; lower extremity length is equivalent to thigh length plus tibial height.

Reliability

Reliability data for direct thigh length are available for the elderly only (intermeasurer technical error: men 1.24 cm, women 0.88 cm; Chumlea, 1983). The reliability of projected thigh length depends on the reliability of sitting height and of tibial height. The reliability of sitting height is described separately; the reliability of tibial height has not been reported.

Sources of Reference Data

Children
Roche & Malina, 1983

Adults
Clauser et al., 1972
Stoudt et al., 1965

Calf Length

Recommended Technique

Calf length is measured as either (a) the direct length between the knee joint line and the tip of the medial malleolus (see Figure 8) or (b) the projected length, which is the vertical distance from the proximal surface of the tibia to the sole of the foot. An anthropometer is needed to make these measurements.

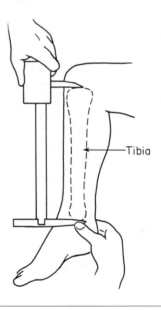

Figure 8 Measurement of direct calf length.

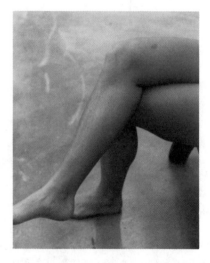

Figure 9 Subject position for direct calf length measurement.

Direct Length. The subject sits and crosses the leg over the opposite knee (see Figure 9). The measurer marks the proximal end of the medial border of the tibia and the distal tip of the medial malleolus (see Figures 10 and 11). The measurer sits or crouches in front of the subject and applies the blades of the anthropometer, fitted as a sliding caliper, so that one is on each landmark. The shaft of the anthropometer is maintained parallel to the long axis of the tibia (Figure 12).

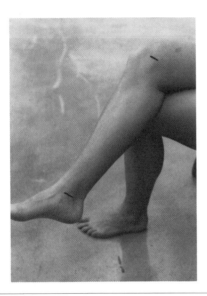

Figure 10 Landmarks for calf length measurement.

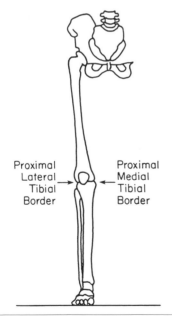

Figure 11 Proximal medial tibial border.

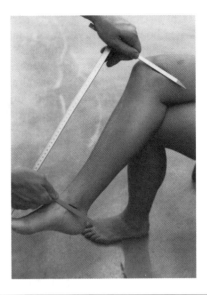

Figure 12 Anthropometer in position for direct calf length measurement.

Projected length. To locate the horizontal lateral border of the proximal end of the tibia, the measurer asks the subject to flex the knee. Then he or she finds the depression bounded by the epicondyle of the femur, the anterolateral portion of the proximal end of the tibia, and the head of the fibula. From this depression, the measurer presses medially, locating the border of the tibia, and then palpates posteriorly along the border to locate the most superior point. This point is at least one third of the distance from the anterior to the posterior surface of the knee joint on its lateral aspect (see Figure 13). The site is on the lateral aspect of the knee joint at the level of the superior surface of the

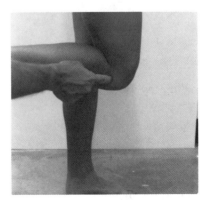

Figure 13 Location of lateral border of the proximal end of tibia for projected calf length measurement.

tibia but is not superficial to the tibia. When the landmark has been identified, the subject stands erect, and a mark is made at the site (see Figure 14). Standing at the side of the subject, the measurer holds the anthropometer shaft vertically, with its base on the floor, and slides the blade down until it touches the marked site (see Figure 15). The caliper is read to the nearest 0.1 cm.

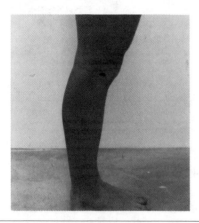

Figure 14 Landmark for lateral border of the proximal end of the tibia is marked.

Figure 15 Anthropometer in position for direct calf length measurement.

Purpose

Calf length is one of the lower extremity segment lengths. It is useful in studies of body proportions and of human engineering.

Literature

Projected calf length can best be measured using a Martin (GPM) type anthropometer, preferably equipped with a base plate to help keep it vertical (Carter et al., 1982; Ross & Marfell-Jones, 1983). Direct calf length is measured using a Harpenden or Martin anthropometer assembled as a large sliding caliper (Cameron, 1984). Special calipers may be used (Behnke & Wilmore, 1974; Chumlea, 1985). The recently developed Mediform caliper is slightly more accurate than the Harpenden caliper (Chumlea, 1985).

Projected calf length is usually measured as part of a sequence of measures of bony landmark heights from superior to inferior while the subject holds a static, erect posture (Martin & Saller, 1959; Ross & Marfell-Jones, 1983). In this sequence, the lateral location of the site facilitates the measurement because the anthropometer is to the outside of the subject; otherwise the sagittal outline of some subjects would interfere with the vertical alignment of the instrument. A site on the medial aspect of the knee has been described (Clauser, 1972; Martin & Saller, 1959; Weiner & Lourie, 1981). Hertzberg et al. (1963) commented that they planned to mark the level of the proximal end of the tibia on the medial aspect of the knee, but their subjects were so "sinewy" that this was abandoned as too difficult to locate with certainty. If the tibial plateau is horizontal, there will be no difference between the levels of the medial and lateral sites in this area, but there will be differences in the presence of knock knees or bow legs.

Knee height (Chumlea et al., 1984a; Hertzberg et al., 1963), inferior patellar height, and popliteal height (Clauser et al., 1972; Hertzberg et al., 1963) are examples of measures similar to, but not identical with, calf length. Calf length can be derived also as the difference between tibial height and medial malleolus height. The recommended positioning for the direct measurement of calf length is based on the description by Cameron (1983).

Reliability

In elderly persons, the intermeasurer technical errors were 0.39 cm (men) and 0.68 cm (women) in an unpublished study by Chumlea (1983).

Sources of Reference Data

Children
Ross & Marfell-Jones, 1983

Adults
Clauser et al., 1972

Arm Span

Recommended Technique

The method requires a tape at least 2 m long, a flat surface (usually a wall), and an adjustable block that is fixed to the wall. The spool of the tape is fixed to the adjustable block. The block serves as the contact point for the middle (longest) finger of the right hand, which is in contact with it when the subject is positioned. The block must be movable so that it can be adjusted vertically to accomodate individuals of varying statures. The block is adjusted to bring the tape to the shoulder level for the subject, and then the tape is pulled horizontally along the wall. The subject stands with the feet together and so that his or her back is against the wall. The arms are outstretched laterally and maximally at the level of the shoulders, in contact with the wall, and with the palms facing forwards. The tip of the middle (longest) finger (excluding the fingernail) of the right hand is kept in contact with the block, while the zero end of the tape is set at the tip of the middle (longest) finger (excluding the fingernail) of the left hand (see Figures 16 and 17). Two measurers are necessary, one at the

Figure 16 Subject positioning for arm span measurement.

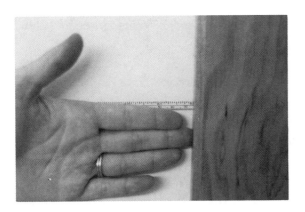

Figure 17 Measurement of arm span showing tip of longest fingers in contact with block.

zero end of the tape and the other at the block end to make the reading. The measurement is recorded to the nearest 0.1 cm. Occasionally a small stool may be required to make this measurement in tall subjects.

When making this measurement, it is imperative that the subject's arms be outstretched maximally and that they are held in this position until the reading is taken. Young children and older individuals tend to lower the arms.

Purpose

Arm span is the distance between the tips of the middle (longest) fingers of each hand (excluding the fingernails) when both arms are extended laterally and maximally to the level of the shoulders. This composite measurement includes both upper extremities and the breadth across the shoulders. Arm span is highly correlated with stature and, thus, may have clinical relevance when stature or recumbent length cannot be measured. Arm span is occasionally used to estimate stature at maturity in the elderly, that is, stature in young adulthood before age-associated stature loss has occurred (Rossman, 1979). In addition, there is considerable kyphosis in some elderly individuals and, as a result, an accurate measure of stature is not possible. Arm span-stature differences may be altered in some clinical syndromes (Engstrom et al., 1981). Hence, arm span in conjunction with stature may be useful in clinical diagnosis.

The relation between arm span and stature varies between American blacks and whites. The differences between means of arm span and stature are larger in black than in white adults (Davenport, 1921; McPherson et al., 1978). Similar differences are evident for projected arm length and stature in American black and white children and youth (Krogman, 1970). This is indirect evidence for corresponding racial differences in the arm span-stature relation during growth.

Data for changes in arm span and for arm span-stature relation during growth are not extensive. Serial data for Australian children of British ancestry indicate greater mean differences between arm span and stature in boys than in girls at all ages between 8 and 15 years (Engstrom et al., 1981). Arm span is, on the average, greater than stature at all ages in boys. In girls, however, stature is slightly greater than arm span before 11.5 years, whereas the reverse is true at older ages (Engstrom et al., 1981).

It is often assumed that arm span and stature are approximately equal in young adulthood. This appears to be so, on the average, in young white women, but not in young black women (Steele & Mattox, unpublished data), and in a small sample of Belgian women in their 30s and 40s (Dequeker et al., 1969). At older ages, arm span is, on the average, greater than recumbent length in white women, and the difference between the two measurements increases progressively with age (Brown & Wigzell, 1964; Dequeker et al., 1969). Among American black men and women, however arm span is, on the average, greater than recumbent length in all age groups between 50 and 90+ years (McPherson et al., 1978). Corresponding data for small samples of American white men and women in the study by McPherson et al. (1978) are not consistent with observations on elderly whites in the same study, or with data for hospital patients (Brown & Wigzell, 1964), and Belgian women (Dequeker et al., 1969).

Literature

The recommended procedure is based on that used by Engstrom et al. (1981). An alternative is to have the zero point of the tape in a corner, where two walls come together. The measurement is then taken from the side wall to the tip of the middle (longest) finger of the other hand after the subject is positioned as described above. An important feature of the arm-span measurement is the need to adjust the height of the tape to the subject's shoulder height. This is especially necessary when measuring children, among whom stature varies considerably. Thus, a vertically adjustable system is essential.

With adults, the range of shoulder heights can be estimated, and a millimeter scale can be affixed to the wall. In a Norwegian study, for example, "A piece of millimeter paper, 40 cm. in breadth, [was] fastened on the wall in such a position that it [formed] a tape measure on the wall with 'zero' in the corner at the cross-wall" (Udjus, 1964, cited in Garrett & Kennedy, 1971). With the subject properly positioned, the reading can be taken directly off the paper. The paper, of course, would be subject to wear and tear, and would probably be influenced by humidity. A plastic cover over properly affixed or laminated millimeter paper would reduce wear-and-tear effects.

Arm span can be measured with the subject supine, and the available data for adults have been collected in this manner (Brown & Wigzell, 1964; Dequeker et al., 1969; McPherson et al., 1978; Steele & Mattox, unpublished data). Each subject was supine on a flat surface with the feet together and the arms extended maximally and horizontally at the level of the shoulders. The measurement was made with a type of anthropometer (the cited studies refer to a "measuring stick" and do not indicate whether the palms faced upward). If arm span is to be measured supine, the fixed end of an anthropometer is placed at the tip of the middle (longest) finger of one hand, while the movable arm is set on the tip of the middle (longest) finger of the other hand, excluding the fingernails. The anthropometer is positioned so that it passes just over the clavicles. Two measurers are necessary to make the reading, one at the fixed end of the anthropometer and the other at the movable end. Measurements of arm span must be made with the subjects supine between birth and 2 or 3 years of age.

Deformity of an extremity or the presence of a contracture limits the validity of the measurement of arm span. Several investigators measure the distance from the "sternal notch" to the tip of the longest finger of the unaffected extremity and double this value to estimate arm span (Brown & Wigzell, 1964; Dequeker et al., 1969; Engelbach, 1932; McPherson et al., 1978). The sternal notch is not defined by these authors, but presumably it is the most superior point on the sternum in the midline (Hrdlička, 1939), or the deepest point in the suprasternal notch (Olivier, 1969). This procedure provides an estimate that does not take individual asymmetry into consideration.

Reliability

In the elderly the intermeasurer technical errors are 0.56 cm for men and 0.38 cm for women (Chumlea, 1983).

Sources of Reference Data

Children
Engstrom et al., 1981
Wolański et al., 1975

Adults
Dequeker et al., 1969
Gleń et al., 1982
McPherson et al., 1978
Wolański et al., 1975

Shoulder-Elbow Length

Recommended Technique

This measurement is made using an anthropometer configured as a sliding-beam caliper. The subject wears clothes that allow the body position to be seen. The shoulders and arms are bare. The subject stands erect on a flat surface with his or her weight distributed evenly on both feet, the head positioned in the Frankfort Plane and the line of sight horizontal.

The shoulders and upper arms are relaxed, with the shoulders drawn back and the upper arms hanging loosely at the subject's sides. Weight is distributed equally between the feet. Both elbows are flexed to place the ulnar surfaces of the forearms and the hands in the horizontal plane and parallel to each other (see Figure 18). The subject breathes normally.

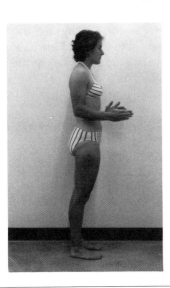

Figure 18 Subject position for shoulder-elbow length measurement.

The beam of the anthropometer is positioned parallel to the posterior aspect of the arm. While maintaining the fixed blade of the anthropometer in firm contact with the superolateral aspect of the acromion, the measurer moves the sliding blade of the anthropometer into firm contact with the posterior surface of the olecranon process of the ulna (see Figure 19). The measurement, which is the distance between the landmarks projected parallel to the longitudinal axis of the upper arm, is recorded to the nearest 0.1 cm

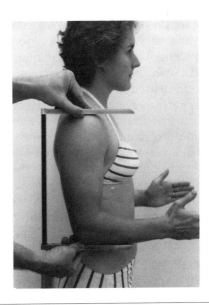

Figure 19 Anthropometer in position for shoulder-elbow length measurement.

Purpose

Shoulder–elbow length is applied in human engineering studies of workspace design (e.g., location of hand controls), and in biomechanical analyses of human motion (e.g., composition and resolution of forces acting within or on the body, during movement or at rest). It is used also to generate limb-segment models of man. Functionally, the axes of rotation of the shoulder are not located at the junction of the humerus and scapula, but lie within the head of the humerus, and the joint axis shifts as the arm moves in space. In contrast, the axis of rotation of the elbow joint is proximal to its articular surfaces. Therefore, the relationships of surface anthropometric landmarks to the shoulder and elbow joint centers must be predetermined for functional analyses employing this measure.

Literature

Shoulder–elbow length should be measured with a portable anthropometer configured as a sliding-beam caliper, having a metric rule, a fixed blade, and a sliding blade. This instrument allows measurement of the distance from the acromion to the olecranon, with minimal effect of adipose and muscular tissue. Measurements using this equipment have been reported in most anthropometric studies (Garrett & Kennedy, 1971; Hertzberg et al., 1963; Roebuck et al., 1975).

One source (MacDonald et al., 1978) cites the use of two walls, at 90° to each other, to measure upper arm length. Using this technique, the subject stands with the scapulae touching the rear wall. The measured arm is extended so that the forearm is horizontal and parallel to the side wall. The recorded measure spans the horizontal distance from the olecranon process to the rear wall. This measure may be a good functional descriptor of arm length, but it restricts use of the data to human engineering applications such as hand-control placement. The data obtained are not equivalent to those obtained with an anthropometer.

The recommended positioning follows the method favored by most workers (Garrett & Kennedy, 1971). The elderly and the young may require assistance to maintain this position.

There is disparity in the definitions of the acromion landmark. In many instances, it has not been described at all (Garrett & Kennedy, 1971). In other reports, it is referred to as the lateral protrusion of the lateral edge of the acromial spine, the lateral point on the superior surface of the acromion process, the highest point on the lateral edge of the acromial spine, the top of the acromion process, or the outer point of the shoulder (Garrett & Kennedy, 1971; Stewart, 1985). To standardize this landmark, it is recommended that the most lateral point on the superior surface of the acromion process, as determined by palpation, be used.

Measurement of shoulder–elbow length can be made with the subject sitting or standing. However, if other arm measurements are to be made in addition to shoulder–elbow length (e.g., elbow–wrist length, hand length), a standing posture is recommended for all of these related measurements. A vertical mirror, placed directly in front of the subject, aids to establish a horizontal line of sight and can assist the subject's maintenance of a stable upright posture, either standing or sitting.

Reliability

Test-retest data from the 1985 survey of 530 Canadian Forces aircrew resulted in estimates for the intrameasurer and intermeasurer variance of 2.7 and 8.4 mm², respectively (Stewart, 1985).

Sources of Reference Data

Children
Krogman, 1970

Malina et al., 1973
Snyder et al., 1975

Adults
National Aeronautics and Space Administration, 1978
Hertzberg et al., 1963
Stewart, 1985

Elbow-Wrist Length

Recommended Technique

Elbow-wrist length is measured with a sliding caliper. The subject wears clothing that permits body positioning to be observed. The arms and shoulders are bare. The subject, unsupported by a wall or similar structure, stands erect on a flat horizontal surface with heels together, weight equally distributed between both feet, and the shoulders drawn back. The subject breathes normally with the head in the Frankfort Plane.

The subject's arms hang by the sides. The elbows are flexed to 90°, and the palms face medially, with the fingers extended in the direction of the long axes of the forearms. The very young and the elderly may need assistance to maintain this position.

The fixed arm of the caliper is positioned to make firm contact with the most posterior point overlying the olecranon, while the sliding arm of the caliper is aligned with the most distal palpable point of the styloid process of the radius (see Figures 20 and 21). During this measurement, the arms of the sliding caliper are held perpendicular to the long axis of the forearm. The measurement is recorded to the nearest 0.1 cm.

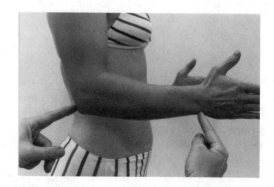

Figure 20   Landmarks for elbow-wrist length measurement.

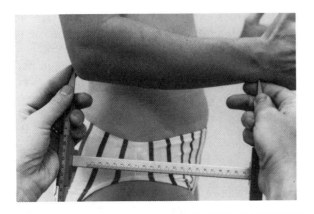

Figure 21 Sliding caliper in position for elbow-wrist length measurement.

Purpose

Limb and limb-segment lengths are important in human biomechanics and in the application of anthropometric data to workspace design, including the construction of anthropometric human-form models. Elbow-wrist length, in conjunction with hand length, is used in human-engineering studies of hand-control location.

Literature

Elbow–wrist length has been measured with the elbow flexed at 90° and the posterior surface of the arm in contact with a plane vertical surface, such as is found in anthropometric measuring rigs based on Morant's apparatus (Bolton et al., 1973; MacDonald et al., 1978; Roebuck et al., 1975). Because the measurement is likely to be affected by local adipose and muscular tissues, this method is not considered equivalent to the recommended technique. Also an instrument that makes a point-to-point measurement, such as a spreading caliper, is not equivalent to a sliding caliper for this measurement.

The recommended positioning follows the method favored by most anthropometrists, as reported in Garrett and Kennedy's collation (1971). However, some anthropometrists have measured forearm length, with the arm and forearm hanging vertically (Garrett & Kennedy, 1971). This is not a functional measurement in engineering anthropometry and has no known advantage for other applications over the recommended technique. Methods that measure from a vertical datum plane in contact with the posterior surface of the arm, although arguably more "functional," confound long-bone measurement with soft-tissue measurement. This tends to restrict use of the data to situations where the functional aspect of the dimension is of prime importance, for example, in placing hand controls in relation to a seat back.

This measurement can be made with the subject sitting, but if both shoulder-elbow length and elbow-wrist length are to be measured, a standing posture is recommended. A vertical mirror, placed directly in front of the subject, aids in establishing a horizontal line of sight and, in conjunction with other devices (e.g., a movable sight line; Hendy, 1979), can help the subject maintain a stable upright posture.

Reliability

Test-retest data from the 1985 anthropometric survey of Canadian Forces aircrew resulted in estimates for the intrameasurer and intermeasurer variances of 2.9 and 9.8 mm², respectively (Stewart, 1985). In the elderly, the intermeasurer technical errors were 0.34 cm for men and 0.31 cm for women (Chumlea, 1983).

Sources of Reference Data

Children

Martin, 1955

Adults

National Aeronautics and Space Administration, 1978

Stewart, 1985

Hand Length

Recommended Technique

This measurement is made with a small sliding caliper from the styloid process of the radius to the tip of the middle finger. The subject sits or stands with arms hanging relaxed and the forearms extended horizontally. The subject's hand and fingers, palm up, are extended in the direction of the longitudinal axis of the forearm (see Figure 22). In this position the fingers are together and extended but not hyperextended.

With the bar of the sliding caliper held parallel to the longtidunal axis of the hand, the fixed arm of the caliper is aligned with the most distal palpable point of the styloid process of the radius. The sliding arm of the caliper is placed so that it makes light contact with the fleshy tip of the third (middle) digit (see Figure 22). The measurement is recorded to the nearest 0.1 cm.

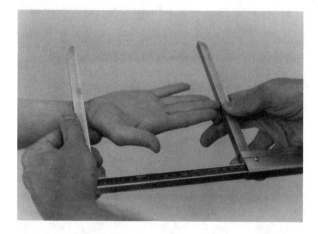

Figure 22 Sliding caliper in place for hand length measurement.

Purpose

Hand length is one of a suite of measurements that can be made on the hand for use in the design of personal clothing items (e.g., gloves) and for workspace layout. In conjunction with forearm-hand length, it may be used to generate a limb-segment anthropometric model of human beings.

Literature

There is a widespread acceptance of the sliding caliper as a measuring device for this dimension. Of the surveys cited in Garrett and Kennedy's collation (1971), in which the measuring instrument for hand length is mentioned, the sliding caliper is universally favored.

The main variation in site location for hand-length measurements concerns the wrist landmark. This has been located at the wrist crease at the base of the hypothenar eminence, the midpoint of a line joining the styloid processes, the midpoint of a line joining the proximal limits of the thenar and hypothenar eminences, and the proximal end of the scaphoid (Garrett & Kennedy, 1971). Garrett (1971) investigated the relation between wrist marks at the distal end of the styloid process of the radius, the proximal edge of the scaphoid, and the major wrist crease. He reported that for 79% of his subjects, the wrist crease lay between the

scaphoid (most proximal) landmark and the styloid (most distal) landmark. Garrett advises the use of wrist-crease landmark because of this central tendency and because of possible difficulties in palpating bony edges in some subjects. However, some patterns of wrist creases make the unequivocal identification of the appropriate landmark extremely difficult. Therefore, despite the difficulty of location by palpation, a skeletal landmark has been selected for the recommended technique rather than a skin crease. The styloid landmark is marginally easier to locate than the scaphoid and is already firmly entrenched as a landmark for elbow-wrist length (Garrett & Kennedy, 1971).

Reliability

Inter- and intrameasurer variability data are not available.

Sources of Reference Data

Children
Pieper & Jürgens, 1977
Simmons, 1944
Snyder et al., 1975

Adults
National Aeronautics and Space Administration, 1978

Forearm-Hand Length

Recommended Technique

This measurement is made with a sliding-beam caliper between the olecranon and the tip of the middle finger. The subject wears clothing that permits the positioning to be observed. The arms and shoulders are bare. The subject, unsupported by a wall or similar structure, stands erect on a flat horizontal surface with heels together (or as close as is possible), weight equally distributed on both feet, shoulders back, breathing normally, and with the head positioned in the Frankfort Horizontal Plane but not rigidly to attention.

The subject's arms are vertical, with the elbows resting lightly against the sides of the body. The elbows are flexed to about 90° so that the forearms and the supinated hands are extended forwards horizontally. The fingers are together and extended in the direction of the longitudinal axes of the forearms (see Figure 23).

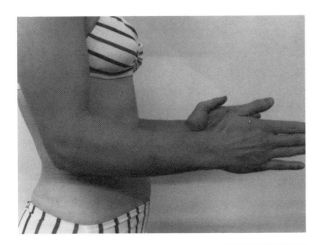

Figure 23 Subject position for forearm-hand length measurement.

The fixed arm of the beam caliper is placed to make firm contact with the most posterior surface overlying the olecranon, while the sliding arm of the caliper is shifted to make contact with the fleshy tip of the third digit (middle finger) of the extended hand (see Figure 24). During this measurement, the arms of the sliding caliper are perpendicular to the longitudinal axis of the forearm. The measurement is recorded to the nearest 0.1 cm.

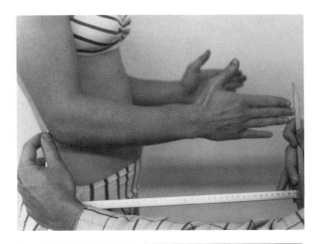

Figure 24 Sliding caliper in place for forearm-hand length measurement.

Purpose

Limb and limb-segment lengths are important to those concerned with human biomechanics and the application of anthropometric data to workspace design and analysis. Forearm-hand length is used in human-engineering studies of hand-

control location and, in conjunction with hand length, can generate a limb-segment anthropometric model of human beings.

Literature

Forearm-hand length has been measured with the elbow flexed at 90° and the posterior surface of the arm in contact with a plane vertical surface (Bolton et al., 1973; McDonald et al., 1978), as is found in anthropometric measuring rigs based on Morant's apparatus (Roebuck et al., 1975). Because this measurement is likely to be affected by the amount of local adipose and muscular tissue, this method is not equivalent to the recommended technique. Also an instrument that makes a point-to-point measurement, such as a spreading caliper, is not equivalent to the beam caliper for the measurement of this dimension.

The recommended positioning generally follows that favored by most anthropometrists (Garrett & Kennedy, 1971). However, supination of the hand is a variation intended to avoid complications that may be introduced if the subject has long fingernails. Some anthropometrists have made a forearm-length measurement with the arm and forearm hanging vertically (Garrett & Kennedy, 1971). This is not a functional measurement in engineering anthropometry and has no advantage for other applications over the recommended technique. Methods that measure from a vertical datum plane that is in contact with the posterior surface of the arm, although arguably more ''functional,'' confound long-bone measurement with tissue measurement. This tends to restrict the use of the data to those situations where the functional aspect of the dimension is of prime importance, for example, in placing hand controls in relation to a seat back.

Forearm–hand length can be measured with the subject sitting. However, if both forearm–hand length and shoulder-elbow length are to be measured, a standing posture is recommended for both measurements. A vertical mirror, placed directly in front of the subject, helps establish a horizontal line of sight and, in conjunction with other devices (e.g., a movable sight line; Hendy, 1979), can assist the subject to maintain a stable upright sitting or standing posture.

Reliability

Intrameasurer and intermeasurer variability data are not available.

Sources of Reference Data

Children

Verghese et al., 1969

Adults

National Aeronautics and Space Administration,
  1978
Stewart, 1985

Chapter 3

Body Breadth Equipment and Measurement Techniques

Jack H. Wilmore,

Roberto A. Frisancho,

Claire C. Gordon,

John H. Himes,

Alan D. Martin,

Reynaldo Martorell, and

Vernon D. Seefeldt

Body breadth measurements are used for several research and clinical purposes. Body breadths are used in the determination of body types, for example, the Heath-Carter somatotyping technique (1967); in determining frame size for estimating desirable weight from standard stature-weight charts, and in estimating the potential for lean weight gains in various populations, for example, athletes and anorexics.

Body breadths are typically measured by special calipers that vary according to the body segment being measured. Generally, narrow or broad blade anthropometers are used to measure the breadth of large segments, for example, biacromial or bitrochanteric breadths. Smaller sliding calipers are preferred to measure the breadth of small segments, for example, elbow and wrist, but spreading calipers can be used effectively if care is taken to keep the line between the tips oriented as recommended for the particular measure. Special spreading calipers may be used to measure chest depth, for which the standard anthropometer is awkward.

From a review of the research literature over the past 20 years, the Siber-Hegner (#101) anthropometer appears to be the instrument used most frequently. This Martin-type anthropometer consists of a rod comprised of four sections and two blades. One blade is fixed, and the other moves along the rod, which is calibrated in centimeters and millimeters. For most breadths, a single section, as opposed to all four sections, can be used. The minimum measurement obtainable is 0.4 cm, the maximum is 210 cm, with an accuracy of 0.5 cm (Chumlea, 1985). The Holtain anthropometer has a minimum measurement of 5 cm and a maximum measurement of 57 cm, with an accuracy of 0.1 cm (Chumlea, 1985). The Mediform anthropometer has a minimum measurement of 0 cm, a maximum measurement of 80 cm, and an accuracy of 0.05 cm (Chumlea, 1985).

The small sliding caliper (Siber-Hegner #104 or the Fisher precision caliper) consists of a flat metal bar upon which a slide moves. It is calibrated in centimeters and millimeters, and one blade is fixed while the other moves. Spreading calipers (Siber-Hegner #106) are configured to allow measurements between landmarks that would be difficult with standard anthropometers. Figure 1 illustrates a standard anthropometer, Figure 2 shows a small sliding caliper, and Figure 3 displays a spreading caliper. All calipers should be maintained careful-

27

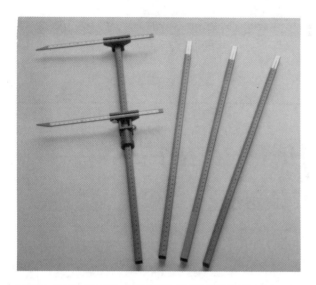

Figure 1 A standard anthropometer with extension rods.

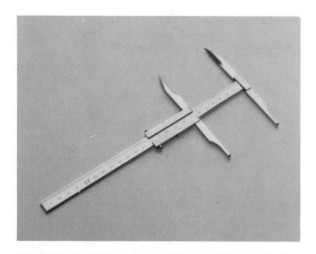

Figure 2 A small sliding caliper.

ly to assure smooth sliding of the caliper arms, and their calibration should be checked regularly. Calibration is particularly important with spreading calipers, which are made of soft metal that is easily distorted.

Body breadth sites are typically defined by bony landmarks. It is important to select landmarks that are palpable not only in lean but also in obese individuals. The anthropometer or caliper is held so that the tips of the index fingers are adjacent to the tips of the projections of the anthropometer/caliper. The landmarks are first identified by the tips of the index fingers and then the projections of the anthropometer/caliper are positioned at those points. Sufficient pressure should be applied to assure that the blades of the anthropome-

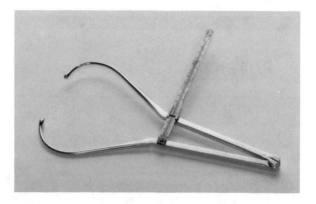

Figure 3 A spreading caliper.

ter/caliper are measuring bony breadths and that the underlying muscle, fat, and skin make minimal contributions to the obtained dimensions. For most sites, firm pressure to the point where the measurement is stable (that is, it does not continue to decrease as pressure is applied) is mandatory. A minimum of three measurements should be obtained for each site, but the second and third measurements should be obtained sequentially, not consecutively, to avoid experimenter bias.

Biacromial Breadth

Recommended Technique

Biacromial breadth is measured from the rear of the subject, because this allows the measurer to locate the acromial processes with ease. The subject stands, because sitting interferes with the posture required for measurement. The heels of the subject are together as in the measurement of stature, and the arms hang by the sides. The shoulder region should be free of clothes. The position of the shoulders is of great importance. The objective is to have the subject relaxed with the shoulders downward and slightly forward so that the reading is maximal. For tall subjects, a measurer should use a stool to allow accurate reading of the anthropometer.

Standing directly behind the subject, the measurer runs his or her hands from the base of the neck outwards to the tips of the shoulders, relaxing any tension. The most lateral borders of the acromial processes (see Figure 4) are palpated and, holding the anthropometer so that its blades are between the index and middle fingers and resting on the base of the thumb, the blades are applied firmly to the most lateral borders of the acromial

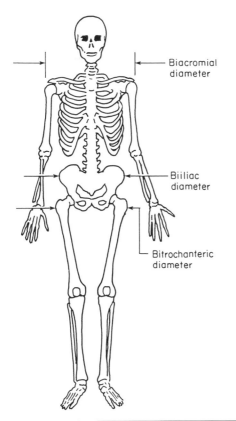

Figure 4 Illustration of locations of biacromial, biiliac and bitrochanteric diameters.

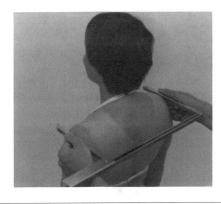

Figure 5 Anthropometer in place for biacromial breadth measurement.

processes (see Figure 5). The width is read to the nearest 0.1 cm.

Purpose

Biacromial breadth is often measured as an index of body frame. It is also useful in somatotyping and in the evaluation of sex-associated differences in physique. This measurement is relevant to the design of clothing and work spaces.

Literature

Although the lateral projections of the acromial processes are easily palpable, the measurement has large errors if the shoulders are not positioned properly. If the shoulders are braced back, the measurement is reduced by 2 to 3 cm (Cameron, 1978; Harrison et al., 1964). Faulhaber (1970), noted large interobserver error variances due to marked differences in "the observers' ability to get the subjects to square their shoulders."

There is agreement that biacromial breadth should be measured from the rear (Cameron, 1978; Tuddenham & Snyder, 1954; Weiner & Lourie, 1981), but Behnke and Wilmore (1974) include a photograph showing the measurement being taken from the front. Cameron (1978) states that the measurer should sit or stand directly behind the subject.

An aspect of considerable importance is the amount of pressure applied in making the measurement. The recommendation of Behnke and Wilmore (1974), Cameron (1978), Weiner and Lourie (1981), and Ross and Marfell-Jones (1983) is to apply firm pressure so as to compress the soft tissues.

Reliability

The intrameasurer and intermeasurer technical errors for biacromial diameter in children are about 0.1 to 0.7 cm (Buschang, 1980; Malina, 1968; Meleski, 1980; Zavaleta, 1976).

In college-aged males the test-retest correlation for measurements made the same day was 0.92 (Wilmore & Behnke, 1969). In adults measured 5 years apart, the test-restest correlation for biacromial breadth was 0.83 (Friedlander et al., 1977). Chumlea et al. (1984b) reported a technical error of measurement of 0.48 cm for male senior citizens, 1.15 cm for female senior citizens, and 0.29 cm for younger adult subjects. The population standard deviation is about 2.2 cm (Friedlander et al., 1977); hence, the ratio of the technical error variance to the population variance, an indicator of the relative magnitude of the error variance (Martorell et al., 1975), is low for male senior citizens and for adult subjects (0.05 and 0.02 respectively) but high for female senior citizens (0.27). Other than for the anomalously high error variances for the subsample of female senior citizens, the measurement of biacromial width appears to have high reliability.

Sources of Reference Data

Children

McCammon, 1970
Roche & Malina, 1983
Snyder et al., 1975

Adults

Clauser et al., 1972
Stoudt et al., 1970

Chest Breadth and Depth

Recommended Techniques

Chest Breadth. The measurement of chest breadth requires a large spreading caliper. The subject stands erect, with the feet at shoulder width and the arms slightly abducted to allow easy access to the measurement site. The measurer stands directly in front of the subject (see Figure 6). The measurement is made with the tips of the caliper on the sixth ribs, in the midaxillary line.

Upon palpation of each sixth rib, the measurer places the caliper tips directly on the ribs, with his or her fingers just beneath the caliper tips to prevent them from slipping into intercostal spaces. Very light pressure is applied. The sixth ribs in the

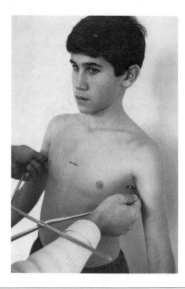

Figure 7   Location of chest breadth landmarks at level of the sixth rib.

midaxillary line correspond, anteriorly, to the fourth costo-sternal joints (see Figure 7). Location of the fourth costo-sternal joints is described in the section on chest circumference. A line is then drawn on the sternum between these junctions.

Chest breadth is measured with the caliper tips in a horizontal plane, at the end of a normal expiration to the nearest 0.1 cm.

Chest Depth. The measurement of chest depth requires a large spreading caliper. The measurement is made with the subject in a natural standing position, arms at the sides. The measurer locates the fourth costo-sternal joints by using the two-handed palpation method described in the section on chest circumference. A line is then drawn horizontally on the sternum between these junctions (see Figure 8).

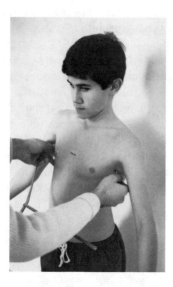

Figure 6   Subject position for measurement of chest breadth.

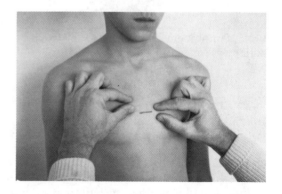

Figure 8   Line drawn on sternum at level of fourth costo-sternal joints.

The measurer stands at the right side of the subject. One tip of the caliper is placed on the sternum in the midline at the level of the fourth costo-sternal junctions. The other tip is placed on the spinous process of the vertebra that is in the same horizontal plane. The measurement is made at the end of the normal expiration to the nearest 0.1 cm (see Figure 9).

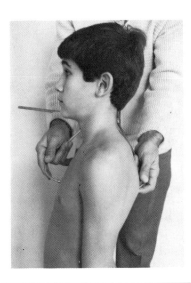

Figure 9 Spreading caliper in place for chest depth measurement.

Purpose

Chest breadth and chest depth are used as indices of growth in children and adolescents, as measures of body size in human engineering to determine appropriate sizes of workspaces, clothing and implements, and as measures of functional capacity in physical performance and in screening tests for respiratory function.

Literature

Many investigators use the anthropometer as a sliding caliper for both breadth and depth measures (Behnke & Wilmore, 1974; De Garay et al., 1974; Malina et al., 1973). Nevertheless, Bailey (1967) and Ross and Marfell-Jones (1982) used a spreading caliper for depth, whereas Montagu (1960) recommended a spreading caliper for both measures.

The techniques used in measuring chest breadth have varied considerably. Orientation of the anthropometer has usually been horizontal for both breadth and depth measures, but some have angled the caliper arms postero-inferiorly for chest breadth, presumably to avoid unusually large latissimus dorsi muscles (Garrett & Kennedy, 1971). It is assumed, and sometimes explicitly stated (Weiner & Lourie, 1981), that the arms of the anthropometer or caliper should rest over the rib surfaces, not the intercostal spaces.

Another source of variation is the pressure with which the anthropometer is applied. Many prefer light contact without soft tissue compression (Olivier, 1969; Weiner & Lourie, 1981). The alternative approach, firm rib contact with soft tissue compression, is frequently termed *chest breadth/depth—bone* (Garrett & Kennedy, 1971).

Chest breadth and depth are most frequently measured at the level of the nipple, with the inferior angles of the scapulae used as posterior landmarks (Garrett & Kennedy, 1971). Variation in the location of the nipples in women, relative to skeletal landmarks, renders this location unreliable. Instead, the superior border of the fourth chondro-sternal joint is frequently substituted for the nipple landmark in women, or in both genders (Comas, 1960; Hertzberg, 1968; Hrdlička, 1920; Olivier, 1969; Weiner & Lourie, 1981). Other observers have measured the chest at the xiphoid level, high in the axilla, or where a maximum reading was obtained (Frisancho & Baker, 1970; Garrett & Kennedy, 1971; Montagu, 1960; Olivier, 1969).

Intraindividual variation in chest size during inspiration and expiration further complicates the measuring techniques used for chest breath or depth. Some measure at maximum expiration and maximum inspiration and calculate a mean of the two values (Frisancho, 1976; Montagu, 1960). Others measure only once at either maximum expiration (Olivier, 1969; Weiner & Lourie, 1981) or maximum inspiration (Laubach et al., 1977).

Reliability

Cameron (1978) placed the measurement of chest depth in the category of "medium consistency," with a coefficient of variation of 1.9%.

Sources of Reference Data

Children

Malina et al., 1973
Morris et al., 1980
Snyder et al., 1975

Adults

Borkan et al., 1981

Biiliac Breadth

Recommended Technique

Synonyms for this measure are *bicristal* or *biilocristal breadth, transverse pelvic breadth*, and *pelvic breadth*. An anthropometer with straight blades is needed to make the measurement. The measurement is made from the rear; this allows easy palpation of landmarks. The subject stands with the feet about 5 cm apart to prevent swaying. The arms need to be away from the area of measurement, preferably folded across the chest (see Figure 10). The anthropometer blades are brought into contact with the iliac crests so that the maximum breadth is recorded. The anthropometer is applied at a downward angle of 45° with firm pressure. The measurement is recorded to the nearest 0.1 cm (Figure 10). During infancy, this measurement must be made with the subject supine.

Figure 10 Anthropometer in place for biiliac breadth measurement.

Purpose

Biiliac breadth is frequently included as an index of frame size, and it is a widely used measure of pelvic size.

Literature

It is generally recommended that the subject stand with heels together and with arms folded or abducted (Cameron, 1978). Children too young to stand in the recommended position are measured when supine.

There is considerable difference of opinion in the literature regarding the amount of pressure to be exerted with the blades of the anthropometer on the landmarks (Cameron, 1978). Most authors state that the measurement of the biiliac width requires the application of more pressure than does biacromial width because of the greater deposition of fat over the pelvic area, particularly in females (Behnke & Wilmore, 1974; Cameron, 1978; Harrison et al., 1964; Weiner & Lourie, 1981). The measurement is difficult in obese subjects. Olivier (1969) states that very light pressure should be applied so that there is no compression, but this is inappropriate for a skeletal dimension.

The caliper is best applied at a downward angle of 45° to separate and compress the tissues (Cameron, 1978; Ross & Marfell-Jones, 1983; Weiner & Lourie, 1981). Most prefer the measurement to be made from the rear (Cameron, 1978; Weiner & Lourie, 1981), but Ross and Marfell-Jones (1983) measure from the front, which they consider preferable, particularly in the obese.

Reliability

In children, the intrameasurer and intermeasurer technical errors vary from 0.1 to 0.6 cm. (Buschang, 1980; Malina, 1968; Meleski, 1980; Zavaleta, 1976). In adults measured 5 years apart, the test-retest correlation was .85 for biiliac breadth (Friedlander et al., 1977). A test-retest correlation of .97 was reported by Wilmore and Behnke (1969) for measurements made the same day in college age males. Chumlea et al. (1984b) reported a technical error of measurement of 0.39 cm for male senior citizens, 0.29 cm for female senior citizens, and 0.38 cm for adult subjects. The population standard deviation is 1.6 to 1.7 cm (Friedlander et al., 1977). Hence, the ratio of the technical error variance to the population variance, an indicator of the relative magnitude of the error variance (Martorell et al., 1975), is low. It appears that biiliac breadth has a high level of reproducibility when measured carefully.

Meredith and Spurgeon (1980) specify a "pre-set limit" of 0.3 cm between two measures by different observers. If the difference exceeds this limit, more measurements are made. Chumlea et al. (1984b) have used a more liberal limit of 1.0 cm.

Sources of Reference Data

Children

Demirjian & Jeniček, 1972
Roche & Malina, 1983
Simmons, 1944

Adults

National Aeronautics and Space Administration, 1978

Snow et al., 1975

Bitrochanteric Breadth

Recommended Technique

Bitrochanteric breadth is the distance between the most lateral projections of the greater trochanters (see Figure 11). An anthropometer with straight blades is used. The subject stands with the heels together and the arms folded over the chest; the measurer stands behind the subject. The maximum distance between the trochanters is measured (see Figure 11). If an index of frame size is required, considerable pressure must be applied with the anthropometer blades to compress the soft tissues. If the measurement is required to design seating, the subject sits, and gentle pressure is applied. The distance is recorded to the nearest 0.1 cm.

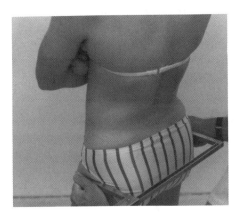

Figure 11 Anthropometer in place for bitrochanteric breadth measurement.

Purpose

The measurent of bitrochanteric breadth is less common than the measurement of biiliac or biacromial breadth as an index of frame size and of fat-free mass. The anthropometric battery proposed by the International Biological Program did not include bitrochanteric breadth (Weiner & Lourie, 1981). If the intent is to obtain a skeletal dimension, as in a study of frame size, firm pressure needs to be exerted. For the design of seating, the objective is to measure the maximum

dimension, including soft tissues. The latter requires that the subject be sitting and that the blades of the anthropometer be applied with minimal pressure.

Literature

Some measure this dimension from the front; others from the back. The only other difference noted in the literature concerns the pressure to be exerted.

Reliability

In children, the intrameasurer and intermeasurer technical errors are 0.1 to 0.3 cm. (Buschang, 1980; Malina, 1968; Meleski, 1980). The test-retest correlation between paired measurements on the same day was .97 for college-aged males (Wilmore & Behnke, 1969). Behnke and Wilmore (1974) state that biacromial, biiliac, and bitrochanteric breadths can be measured with a high degree of reliability because the measurements approximate a bone-to-bone contact, if the soft tissues are compressed. This reduces the variability of repeated measurements and increases accuracy. Less accuracy would be expected in obese subjects and when minimal pressure is applied.

Sources of Reference Data

Children

Roche & Malina, 1983

Adults

National Aeronautics and Space Administration, 1978

Knee Breadth

Recommended Technique

This measurement is defined as the distance between the most medial and most lateral aspects of the femoral condyles (see Figure 12). These points are known as the medial and lateral epicondyles. The leg is flexed 90° at the knee with the subject sitting (see Figure 13). Alternatively, with the subject standing, the leg is flexed 90° at the hip and 90° at the knee, with the foot resting on a suitable raised surface (see Figure 12). The measurer stands facing the subject.

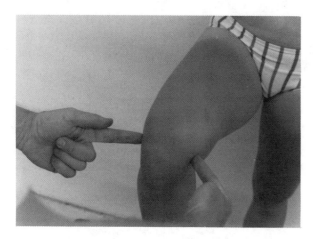

Figure 12 Location of lateral aspects of femoral condyles.

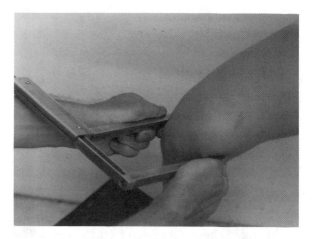

Figure 14 Caliper in place for knee breadth measurement.

Purpose

Knee breadth is commonly used as an indicator of frame size or skeletal mass (Matiegka, 1921; von Döbeln, 1964). Knee breadth is less useful than elbow or wrist breadth in the prediction of skeletal mass probably because of a greater amount of intervening soft tissue at this site (Martin, 1984). Also, it is included in somatotyping based on anthropometry, specifically for the musculoskeletal, or mesomorphic, component (Heath & Carter, 1967; Parnell, 1954).

Literature

The literature shows general agreement regarding the technique to be used. Flexing the leg at the knee minimizes the intrusion of soft tissues into the measurement.

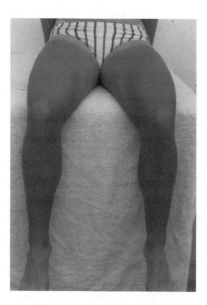

Figure 13 Subject positioning (sitting) for knee breadth measurement.

Reliability

The intra- and intermeasurer technical errors in children are 0.1 to 0.2 cm (Buschang, 1980; Malina, 1968; Meleski, 1980; Zavaleta, 1976). Intraobserver reliability on a small sample ($n = 21$) was very high ($r = .99$; Martin, 1986). Wilmore and Behnke (1969) reported a test-retest correlation of .97 for measurements made the same day in college-aged males.

Sources of Reference Data

Children
Roche & Malina, 1983
Zavaleta, 1976

Using either a sliding or a spreading caliper, the measurer guides the caliper blades or tips with the thumb and index finger of each hand, applying the caliper diagonally downward and towards the subject. The most lateral aspect of the lateral femoral epicondyle is palpated with the index or middle finger of the left hand while the corresponding fingers of the right hand palpate the most medial aspect of the medial epicondyle. The caliper blades or tips are then placed on these points, firm pressure is applied, and the breadth is recorded to the nearest 0.1 cm (see Figure 14). This measurement is not necessarily made in a horizontal plane.

Adults

National Aeronautics and Space Administration, 1978

Clauser et al., 1972

Ankle (Bimalleolar) Breadth

Recommended Technique

The measurement of ankle breadth requires a sliding caliper or a spreading caliper. The barefoot subject stands on a flat surface, with the feet separated about 6 cm and weight evenly distributed on both feet. The subject should stand on an elevated surface to facilitate making the measurement and reading the caliper scale accurately (see Figure 15). The measurer stands behind the subject. Ankle (bi-

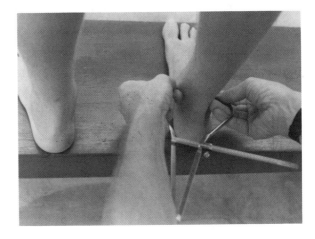

Figure 16 Spreading caliper in place for ankle breadth measurement.

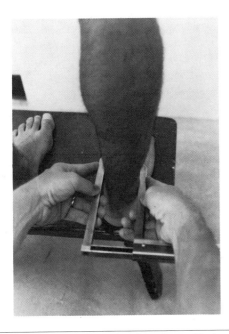

Figure 15 Sliding caliper in place for ankle breadth measurement.

malleolar) breadth should be measured from the posterior aspect of the ankle if there is sufficient ''space'' for the caliper. When the space is insufficient, the measurement can be made from the anterior aspect. The measurement recorded is the maximum distance between the most medial extension of the medial malleolus and the most lateral extension of the lateral malleolus in the same horizontal plane (see Figure 16). A horizontal distance is measured, but the plane between the most medial and most lateral points in this area is ob-

lique, because the lateral malleolus is posteroinferior to the medial malleolus.

Ankle (bimalleolar) breadth is measured with the bar of a sliding caliper perpendicular to the long axis of the foot and near the standing surface, and with the caliper blades slanting upward at an angle of 45° to meet both malleoli at the appropriate measurement points (see Figure 15). If a spreading caliper is used, the line between the tips must be perpendicular to the long axis of the foot (see Figure 16). Sufficient pressure must be applied to compress the tissues overlying the malleoli because the measurement is considered a ''skeletal'' one. Ankle (bimalleolar) breadth is recorded to the nearest 0.1 cm.

When measuring infants and other subjects unable to stand in the appropriate position, the subject should be supine with knees flexed and the soles of the feet flat on the supporting surface.

Purpose

Ankle (bimalleolar) breadth has been proposed as a measure of frame size. It is a weight-bearing joint diameter and is important for interpreting weight-stature relationships because it is correlated with fat-free mass but not with body fat (Himes & Bouchard, 1985).

Literature

Ankle (bimalleolar) breadth can be measured using a sliding caliper or an anthropometer. Spreading calipers are not recommended because they are difficult to position on the malleoli.

Some early workers recommended that the subject stand erect, with heels together. This positioning makes it difficult to measure the dimension. Others have measured ankle (bimalleolar) breadth with the subject sitting on a table (Weiner & Lourie, 1981). Ankle breadth has been reported as the minimum breadth proximal to the malleoli, but this dimension has considerable independence from that measured by the recommended procedure.

Reliability

The intrameasurer technical error for ankle (bimalleolar) breadth in Cycle III of the U.S. Health Examination Survey was 0.92 mm, with a mean difference between replicates of 0.97 mm; corresponding values for the intermeasurer errors were 1.71 mm and 1.86 mm, respectively (Malina et al., 1973). An intraclass reliability coefficient of .94 for replicate measurements has been reported (Himes & Bouchard, 1985).

Sources of Reference Data

Children

Roche & Malina, 1983
Schutte, 1979

Adults

National Aeronautics and Space Administration, 1978
Clauser et al., 1972
Hertzberg et al., 1963

Elbow Breadth

Recommended Technique

The measurement of elbow breadth requires a broad-faced sliding caliper or a small spreading caliper to measure the distance between the epicondyles of the humerus (see Figure 17). The subject raises the right arm to the horizontal, and the elbow is flexed to 90°. The dorsum (back) of the subject's hand faces the measurer. The measurer stands in front of the subject and palpates the lateral and medial epicondyles of the humerus (see Figure 18). If a sliding caliper is used it is then applied pointing the blades upwards to bisect the right angle formed at the elbow. The caliper is held at a slight angle to the epicondyles rather than parallel to them, because the medial epicondyle is

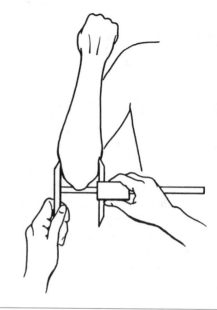

Figure 17   Elbow breadth measurement at the epicondyles of the humerus.

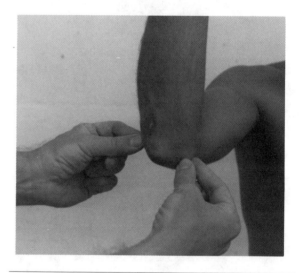

Figure 18   Location of epicondyles of the humerus.

distal to the lateral epicondyle. If a spreading caliper is used, the tips are placed on the medial and lateral epicondyles. The measurer exerts firm pressure to decrease the influence of soft tissue (see Figure 19). The measurement is recorded to the nearest 0.1 cm.

Purpose

Elbow breadth is an index of skeletal mass and has been used as a measure of frame size (Frisancho, 1984).

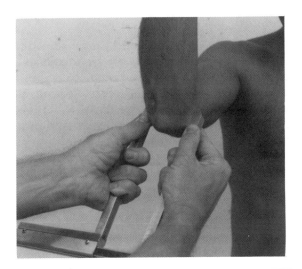

Figure 19 Sliding caliper in place for elbow breadth measurement.

Literature

Firm pressure is exerted so that a skeletal measure will be approximated. Flat-bladed sliding calipers are preferred to spreading calipers because the tips of the latter tend to slip off the bony landmarks. Frisancho (1986) has developed an instrument that consists of a fixed baseboard and a mobile board to measure elbow breadth (see Figure 20).

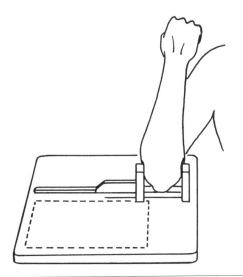

Figure 20 Elbow breadth measures on a fixed baseboard.

Reliability

In children, the intra- and intermeasurer technical errors are about 0.1 cm (Buschang, 1980; Malina

et al., 1972; Malina, 1968; Meleski, 1980; Zavaleta, 1976).

Sources of Reference Data

Children

Johnson et al., 1981
Frisancho, 1986

Adults

Frisancho & Flegel, 1983
Frisancho, 1984

Wrist Breadth

Recommended Technique

The standing subject flexes the forearm 90° at the elbow, keeping the upper arm vertical and near the side of the chest. The measurer stands facing the subject. Guiding the tips of a spreading caliper with the thumb and first finger of each hand, the measurer palpates the most medial aspect of the ulnar styloid with the middle or index finger of the right hand and slides the right tip of the caliper onto this landmark (see Figure 21). Alternate ulnar and radial deviation of the hand at the wrist assists identification of the ulnar and radial styloid processes because they do not move. The most lateral aspect of the radial styloid is located with the middle or index finger of the left hand moving proximally from the space between the extensor pollicis longus and the abductor pollicis longus

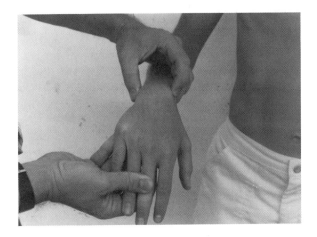

Figure 21 Location of medial aspect of ulna styloid and lateral aspect of radial styloid for the measurement of wrist breadth.

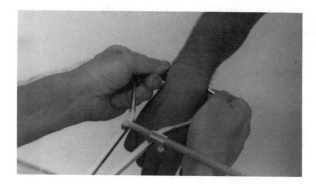

Figure 22 Spreading caliper in place for wrist breadth measurement.

(the anatomical snuff-box; see Figure 22). Alternatively, a sliding caliper can be used to measure the distance between the bony landmarks described above. Firm pressure is applied, and the breadth is recorded to the nearest 0.1 cm.

Purpose

Wrist breadth is used as an index of skeletal mass and of frame size. It has been included in equations for the prediction of skeletal mass (Matiegka, 1921; von Döbeln, 1964). In the Brussels Cadaver Study, wrist breadth was the skeletal measure most highly correlated with skeletal mass (r = .88; Clarys et al., 1984). The value of wrist breadth for this purpose has been confirmed by studies showing it to have low correlations with body fat (Himes & Bouchard, 1985).

Literature

The small contact area of the classical spreading caliper makes positioning on the landmarks difficult. The large flat blades of an adapted engineer's caliper (Carter, 1980) enable accurate placement, and these blades do not shift readily when the necessary pressure is applied, but the scale is difficult to read. A prototype has proved satisfactory, but is expensive and has not been produced in significant quantity (Ross & Marfell-Jones, 1983).

Standardizing wrist positioning is of particular importance because wrist breadth encompasses two bones. The forearm should be midway between pronation and supination, with the dorsum of the hand towards the measurer. Otherwise, there is potential for relative movement of the radial and ulnar styloid processes.

Reliability

Limited data show wrist breadth to be a highly reliable measure with an intrameasurer correlation coefficient of r = .994; n = 16 (Martin, 1986). A test-retest correlation of .96 between paired measurements the same day has been reported for college-aged males (Wilmore & Behnke, 1969).

Sources of Reference Data

Children
Huenemann et al., 1974
Adults
National Aeronautics and Space Administration, 1978
Hertzberg et al., 1963

Chapter 4

Circumferences

C. Wayne Callaway,

William Cameron Chumlea,

Claude Bouchard,

John H. Himes,

Timothy G. Lohman,

Alan D. Martin,

Carol D. Mitchell,

William H. Mueller,

Alex F. Roche, and

Vernon D. Seefeldt

Circumferences are important measurements that record the size of cross-sectional and circumferential dimensions of the body. Circumferences used alone, in combination with skinfold measurements taken at the same location or in combination with other circumferences, are measures of growth and can provide indices of nutritional status and levels of fat patterning. For children younger than 6 years of age, head circumference is an index of brain growth, and the ratio of head circumference to chest circumference is an indirect measure of nutritional status. During later childhood and into adulthood, circumferences of the limbs, together with skinfold measures of subcutaneous adipose tissue thicknesses at corresponding levels, can provide cross-sectional areas of adipose tissue or the areas of the underlying "muscle plus bone." When computed from the appropriate formulae, these areas can be used to monitor levels and changes in amounts of adipose tissue and muscle during nutritional therapy or physical rehabilitation. Ratios between selected circumferences of the trunk and of the limbs can provide indices of the patterning of subcutaneous adipose tissue. These uses of circumferences are detailed in other parts of this manual.

Specific techniques for measuring the circumference of the head, neck, chest, waist, abdomen, hips or buttocks, thigh, calf, ankle, arm, forearm, and wrist are described in the pages that follow. There are several important points common to these techniques. All require the use of a tape measure. The tape measure selected should be flexible but inelastic (nonstretchable), should preferably have only one ruling on a side, (i.e., metric or English), and be about 0.7 cm wide. For the measurement of wrist circumference, the tape must be narrow enough to fit into the depression between the styloid processes of the radius and ulna and the carpals.

Many tapes have a spring-retractable mechanism that is activated by pressing a button. In measuring a circumference with such a tape, the tape should be held so that the retraction spring tension on the tape does not affect the measurement. Some other tapes are designed so that the tension of a spring necessarily affects the measurement; these tapes are not recommended for the measurement of circumferences for which tension should be minimal. Circumferences should be recorded with the zero end of the tape held in the left hand above the remaining part of the tape held by the right hand. Differences within and between observers in this positioning of the zero end of a tape can affect reliability for a measurement.

The positioning of the tape for each specific circumference is important because inconsistent positioning reduces validity and reliability. For each circumference, except those of the head and neck, the plane of the tape around the body is perpendicular to the long axis of that part of the body. For those circumferences typically measured with the subject erect (chest, waist, abdomen, hip, thigh, calf, ankle, arm, and forearm), the plane of the tape is also parallel to the floor. Head circumference is measured as a maximum dimension, whereas neck circumference is measured as a minimum dimension. Techniques for measuring circumferences from subjects in recumbent positions are described in another section of this manual.

The tension applied to the tape by the measurer affects the validity and reliability of the measurements. For head circumference, the tape is pulled tightly to compress the hair and soft tissue of the scalp. For all other circumferences, the tape is held snugly around the body part, but not tight enough to compress the subcutaneous adipose tissue. For these circumferences, the measurer and the recorder should check to ensure that the tape is not indenting the skin. For circumferences of the chest, calf, and arm, there may be gaps between the tape and the skin in some individuals. If the gap is large, a note should be made in the subject's record, but in most instances, this gap is small and of little concern. Attempting to reduce the gap by increasing the tension of the tape is not recommended.

Circumferences appear to be relatively easy measures, but control of intra- and intermeasurer reliability can be difficult. The primary causes of poor reliability are the improper positioning of the tape and differences between measurers in the tension applied. Some error in measures of the trunk may be due to their being made at various phases of respiration. Limits for accepted differences between repeated measures for normal subjects are presented in Table 1. If the limit is exceeded for a pair of intra- or intermeasurer values, an additional pair of measurements should be recorded. Different limits may be needed when individuals who have specific diseases or other abnormal conditions are measured.

Head Circumference

Recommended Technique

An infant is measured when seated on the lap of the mother or caretaker. At older ages, head circumference is measured with the subject standing, but few children less than 36 months old will stand still for this purpose. A nonstretching tape about 0.6 cm wide is used. Added objects, for example, pins, are removed from the hair. The measurer stands facing the left side of the infant and positions the tape so that the zero end is on the lateral aspect of the head (see Figure 1). This involves passing the tape around the head and then transferring the ends of the tape from one hand to the other so that the zero mark on the tape is inferior

Table 1   Intra- and Intermeasurer Limits for Circumferences

Circumference	Limit (cm)
Head	0.2
Neck	0.3
Chest	1.0
Waist	1.0
Abdomen	1.0
Buttocks	1.0
Thigh	0.5
Calf	0.2
Ankle	0.2
Arm	0.2
Forearm	0.2
Wrist	0.2

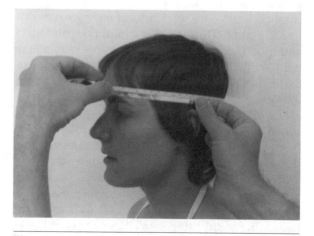

Figure 1   Measurement of head circumference.

to the value to be recorded. The tape is positioned so that large amounts of cranial hair (braids) are excluded. Anteriorly, the tape is placed just superior to the eyebrows and posteriorly it is placed so that the maximum circumference is measured. The tape need not be in the Frankfort Horizontal Plane, but the plane of the tape must be the same on both sides of the head. The tape is pulled tightly to compress hair and obtain a measure that "approximates" cranial circumference. The measurement is recorded to the nearest 0.1 cm.

Purpose

Head circumference is a standard component of infant anthropometry because it is closely related to brain size (Cooke et al., 1977). After 36 months, growth in head circumference is slow although brain weight increases by about 30% after this age. Head circumference should be measured also in the parents of infants whose head circumferences are abnormal because head circumferences of parents and their offspring are closely associated and adjustment equations are available (Illingworth & Eid, 1971).

Literature

There is widespread agreement regarding the technique to be used except that gentle pressure is used by some Dutch workers and in Swedish Infant Welfare Clinics. In addition, a wide tape (2 cm) is used in Swedish Infant Welfare Clinics. Measurements made with a tape 0.6 cm wide are about 0.5 cm smaller than those made with a tape 2 cm wide (Karlberg et al., 1976).

Reliability

In the Fels Longitudinal Study the intermeasurer differences were small and independent of age, with technical errors of 0.09 mm and coefficients of variation of .02 (Roche et al., 1987). Wilmore and Behnke (1969) reported a test-retest correlation of .96 for measurements of young men 1 day apart.

Sources of Reference Data

Children

Nellhaus, 1968
Roche & Himes, 1980
Roche et al., 1987

Adults

Churchill et al., 1977
White & Churchill, 1971

Minimal Neck Circumference

Recommended Technique

The subject does not wear any clothes around the neck and sits or stands erect with the head in the Frankfort Horizontal Plane (see Figure 2). The measurer stands facing the left side of the subject. A self-retracting inelastic tape is applied around the neck just inferior to the laryngeal prominence (Adam's Apple; see Figure 2). The minimal circumference is measured to the nearest 0.1 cm, with the tape perpendicular to the long axis of the neck. The tape will not necessarily be horizontal. The zero mark on the tape should be inferior to the value that will be recorded. The pressure of the tape on the skin should be minimal while maintaining complete contact. The measurement should be made in less than 5 s to avoid discomfort.

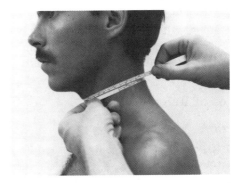

Figure 2 Measurement of minimal neck circumference.

Purpose

Minimal neck circumference can be used in the study of growth, motor and athletic performance, obesity, and aging. The measurement can have useful medical and engineering applications.

Literature

The general concensus is that neck circumference should be measured with the head in the Frankfort Horizontal Plane and should be performed similarly in children and in adults. It has been recommended that neck circumference be measured with the subject standing (Behnke & Wilmore, 1974), but others have recommended a sitting position (Anthropology Research Project, 1978).

In the 1978 Anthropology Research Project "Anthropometric Source Book," the measurement is defined as "the maximum circumference of the neck at a point just inferior to the bulge of the thyroid cartilage" (Volume I: *Anthropometry for Designers*) and later as "the maximum circumference of the neck, including the Adam's Apple" (Volume II: *A Handbook of Anthropometric Data*). Wilmore and Behnke (1969) suggested that this circumference be measured "just inferior to the larynx."

Most have measured at right angles to the long axis of the neck, as is recommended, but some have described the measurement as "taken in the horizontal plane, just below the level of the thyroid cartilage" (Weiner & Lourie, 1981).

Reliability

There are few reliability data. Wilmore and Behnke (1969), from test-retest data for college-aged males, reported that neck circumference was a reliable measurement with an interclass correlation of .95. Gavan (1950) concluded that neck circumference was a measurement of medium reliability.

Sources of Reference Data

Children

Pieper & Jürgens, 1977
Snyder et al., 1975

Adults

Clauser et al., 1972
White & Churchill, 1971

Shoulder Circumference

Recommended Technique

The measurement of shoulder circumference requires that the subject be dressed so that the appropriate landmarks can be located. The subject stands, head erect and looking ahead with weight evenly distributed between both feet, which are about 5 cm apart, and with shoulders back and the arms by the sides (see Figure 3). The measurement

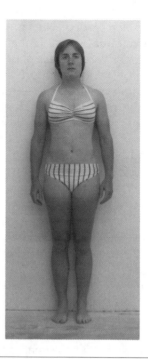

Figure 3 Subject position for shoulder circumference measurement.

is made at the end of a normal expiration. This can be accomplished easily by engaging the subject in light conversation, or by asking that the subject count to 10 during the measurement. The tape is positioned over the maximum muscular bulges (deltoid muscles) inferior to each acromion (see Figure 4). A mirror, or assistant, helps to ensure that the tape is horizontal. The tape is held snug, in contact with the skin, without compressing the tissue. The measurement is recorded to the nearest 0.1 cm.

Purpose

Shoulder circumference reflects muscular development of the shoulder regions and upper thorax.

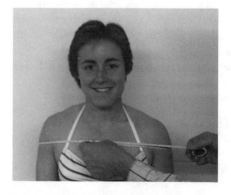

Figure 4 Measurement of shoulder circumference.

Because the deltoid musculature is proportional to lean body mass, shoulder circumferences may indicate changes due to strength training. It is important in human engineering and physical education research.

Literature

Some investigators have defined bony landmarks rather than the maximal protrusion of the deltoid muscles. Circumference measurements are made to estimate the quantity of soft tissue, unlike skeletal breadths and lengths, which estimate frame size. Consequently, the choice of a muscular landmark is appropriate. Also, unlike skeletal measurements, shoulder circumference is measured with little pressure and without compressing the skin (Behnke & Wilmore, 1974). Anteriorly, the tape passes approximately over the junction between the sternum and the second costal cartilage when the recommended technique is followed.

Timing a measurement at the end of a normal expiration is easier to achieve than other timing within the respiratory cycle. It produces less variability between measurements than the choice of other phases of respiration.

Reliability

Reports are not available.

Sources of Reference Data

Children
Huenemann et al., 1974
Adults
National Aeronautics and Space Administration, 1978

Chest Circumference

Recommended Technique

The measurement of chest circumference requires a highly flexible inelastic tape measure that is no more than 0.7 cm wide. During the measurement, the subject stands erect, in a natural manner, with the feet at shoulder width. The arms are abducted slightly to permit passage of the tape around the chest. When the tape is snugly in place, the arms are lowered to their natural postition at the sides of the trunk. The chest should be bare except that women may wear a strapless bra. Chest circumference is measured at the level of the fourth costo-

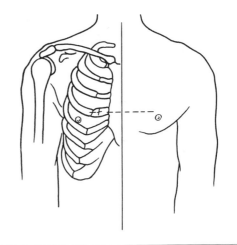

Figure 5 The level of the fourth-sternal joints for chest circumference measurement.

sternal joints (see Figure 5). Laterally, this corresponds to the levels of the sixth ribs. The measurement is made in a horizontal plane, at the end of a normal expiration.

The fourth costo-sternal joints are located by a two-handed palpation method whereby the measurer places both index fingers on the superior surfaces of the clavicles, while the thumbs locate the first intercostal spaces. The index fingers then replace the thumbs, which are lowered to the second intercostal spaces. This procedure is repeated until the fourth ribs are located. The fourth ribs and their costal cartilages are followed medially to their articulations with the sternum. The level of the fourth costo-sternal joints is marked. An alternative procedure is to locate the manubrio-sternal joint, which projects markedly and is at the level of the second costal cartilages. The third and fourth costo-sternal junctions can then be located sequentially.

The measurer stands in front of the subject but slightly to one side. The tape housing is held in the right hand while the free end of the tape is passed in front of the subject and retrieved by the measurer's left hand as it passes around the subject's back. The free end of the tape is then positioned between the right axilla and the sternum. At this time, the measurer ensures that the tape is at the correct horizontal position, first at the back and then at the front. The reserve end of the tape is then placed near the zero end (see Figure 6).

The tape should be in light contact with the skin, without indenting it, but the tape may be away from the skin near the vertebral column. The skin should be free of perspiration, because this may increase friction between the skin and the tape.

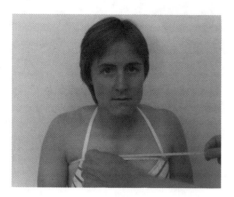

Figure 6 Measurement of chest circumference.

Purpose

In infants and children, chest circumference serves as a screening variable for malnutrition. In children and adults, it can be used as an index of frame size.

Literature

The tape measure should be divided to metric units with unequivocal identification of millimeters and centimeters. There should be a free space between the end of the tape and the zero line to facilitate handling. Spring-loaded tapes are not recommended because they may indent the soft tissues.

Chest circumference has been measured at various sites and at various phases of the respiratory cycle (Behnke & Wilmore, 1974; De Garay et al., 1974; Hrdlička, 1920; Simmons, 1944; Weiner & Lourie, 1981). Consideration was given to the possibility of measuring chest circumference at maximum inspiration and at maximum expiration, which would provide an index of respiratory functional capacity. This is not recommended for general use because it is not applicable to the very young and the elderly, and it does not match the recommended techniques for other thoracic and abdominal dimensions. If all these dimensions were measured at both maximum inspiration and at maximum expiration, many additional measurements would be necessary.

The most frequently mentioned anatomical landmark on the anterior aspect of the thorax is the nipple, which corresponds approximately to the fourth intercostal space (Bailey, 1967; Behnke & Wilmore, 1974; De Garay et al., 1974; Osborne & De George, 1959; Ross & Marfell-Jones, 1982; Singh & Bhasin, 1968). Weiner and Lourie (1981) suggested that the tape be placed at the level of the third and fourth sternebrae, whereas Olivier (1960) recommended a level superior to the nipples.

The position of the tape on the posterior aspect of the thorax is described generally as either crossing the lower angles of the scapulae or passing just distal to them (Bailey, 1967; De Garay et al., 1974; Singh & Bhasin, 1968). Note that when a tape is placed anteriorly at or superior to the nipples and distal to the inferior angles of the scapulae posteriorly, the plane of measurement slopes postero-inferiorly. Alternative levels described in the literature include the xiphoid process (Hrdlička, 1920; Osborne & De George, 1959; Simmons, 1944) and the axilla (Snyder et al., 1975). Ross et al. (1982) recommended that measurements of the chest be made at a midsternal level in a horizontal plane without reference to anatomical landmarks on the posterior aspect of the thorax.

The time of measurement within the respiratory cycle ranges from maximum inspiration and expiration (De Garay et al., 1974; Hrdlička, 1920; Simmons, 1944) to normal or quiet inspiration and expiration (Weiner & Lourie, 1981) and to mid-respiration (Behnke & Wilmore, 1974).

Reliability

Intermeasurer and intertrial reliability coefficients are generally slightly lower than those for limb measures but are well within acceptable ranges. Weltman and Katch (1975) reported intertrial and intermeasurer correlations between .94 and .99. Slaughter, Lohman, and Boileau (1978) reported intertrial correlations greater than .90 for chest circumferences of children from 7 to 12 years of age.

Sources of Reference Data

Children

Meredith, 1970
Malina et al., 1973
Slaughter et al., 1978

Adults

Stoudt et al., 1970
Weltman & Katch, 1975

Waist Circumference

Recommended Technique

The subject wears little clothing so that the tape may be correctly positioned. The measurement should not be made over clothing. If clothing must be worn, subjects should undress to light underwear and wear only a cloth or paper smock during the measurement. The subject stands erect with the abdomen relaxed, the arms at the sides and the feet together. The measurer faces the subject and places an inelastic tape around the subject, in a horizontal plane, at the level of the natural waist, which is the narrowest part of the torso, as seen from the anterior aspect (see Figure 7). An assistant is needed to help position the tape in a horizontal plane. In some obese subjects, it may be difficult to identify a waist narrowing. In such cases, the smallest horizontal circumference should be measured in the area between the ribs and iliac crest. The measurement should be taken at the end of a normal expiration, without the tape compressing the skin. It is recorded to the nearest 0.1 cm.

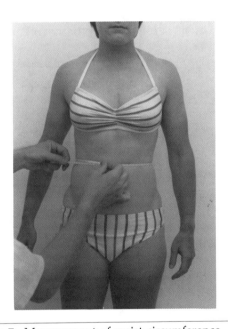

Figure 7   Measurement of waist circumference.

Purpose

Waist circumference is an index of deep adipose tissue (Borkan et al., 1983), and it is related to fat-free mass (Jackson & Pollock, 1976). When used in a ratio with the thigh or buttock (hip) circumference, waist circumference is an indicator of the degree of masculine distribution of adipose tissue: The higher the waist to the thigh or buttock (hip) ratio, the more masculine the pattern of adipose tissue distribution and the greater the risk of diseases such as noninsulin-dependent diabetes mellitus (Hartz et al., 1984; Krotkiewski et al., 1983. Waist circumference is highly correlated with weight/stature² (Kannel & Gordon, 1980), which is an index of general obesity. Waist circumference has important applications in human engineering.

Literature

Waist circumference has usually been measured at the smallest circumference of the torso, which is at the level of the natural waist (Garrett & Kennedy, 1971). Some measure "waist circumference" at the level of the umbilicus, but this leads to recording larger values.

Reliability

The technical error of measurement in adolescents is 1.31 cm for intrameasurer errors and 1.56 cm for intermeasurer errors (Malina et al., 1973). The technical error of measurement in the elderly is 0.48 cm in men and 1.15 cm in women (Chumlea et al., 1984b). Thus, the "true" measurement of an individual would typically be within ± 1 cm of the measured value in most cases.

Sources of Reference Data

Children

Huenemann et al., 1974
Roche & Malina, 1983

Adults

National Aeronautics and Space Administration, 1978
Stoudt et al., 1970

Abdominal Circumference

Recommended Technique

If clothing must be worn, subjects should undress to light underwear and wear only a cloth or paper smock during the measurement. The measurer faces the subject. The subject stands with the arms by the sides and the feet together. The procedures are the same as those to be followed for the waist circumference, except that the tape is placed around the subject at the level of the greatest anterior extension of the abdomen in a horizontal plane. This level is usually, but not always, at the level of the umbilicus (see Figure 8). An assistant is needed to position the tape behind the subject. The tape is held snug against the skin without compressing the tissues and with its zero end below the value to be recorded. The measurement is made at the end of a normal expiration to the nearest 0.1 cm.

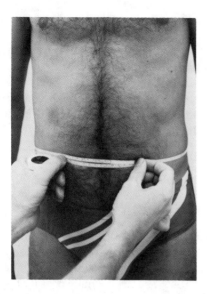

Figure 8 Measurement of abdominal circumference.

Purpose

The abdominal circumference, like the waist circumference, is an anthropometric indicator of subcutaneous and deep adipose tissue. It differs from the waist circumference in being the maximum circumference of the abdomen and, therefore, may be a better indicator of adipose tissue. It is probable that the waist and abdominal circumferences are highly correlated, although the extent is unknown because in most studies one or the other measurement is recorded.

Literature

The recommended procedure is the one used commonly (Behnke, 1963; Hertzbert et al., 1963; Huenemann et al., 1974; Wilmore & Behnke, 1969).

Reliability

Wilmore and Behnke (1969) reported a test-retest correlation of .99 in young men measured 1 day apart.

Sources of Reference Data

Children

Huenemann et al., 1974

Adults

National Aeronautics and Space Administration, 1978
Clauser et al., 1972
Hertzberg et al., 1963

Buttocks (Hip) Circumference

Recommended Technique

The subject should wear only nonrestrictive briefs or underwear, or light smock over underwear. The subject stands erect with arms at the sides and feet together. The measurer squats at the side of the subject so that the level of maximum extension of the buttocks can be seen. An inelastic tape is placed around the buttocks in a horizontal plane at this level without compressing the skin (see Figure 9). An assistant is needed to help position the tape on the opposite side of the subject's body. The zero end of the tape should be below the measurement value. The tape is in contact with the skin but does not indent the soft tissues. The measurement is recorded to the nearest 0.1 cm.

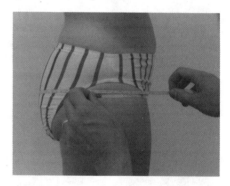

Figure 9 Measurement of buttocks (hip) circumference.

Purpose

Buttocks (hip) circumference is a measurement of external pelvic size that reflects the amount of adipose tissue in the region. As defined, it is more properly called "buttocks circumference" than "hip circumference." Adipose tissue in this region is largely sucutaneous and relates to the lower segment of the body. Hence, buttocks circumference is an indicator of lower body fatness. Used in conjunction with waist circumference, in the waist-to-hip (buttocks) circumference ratio, it is an indicator of the pattern of subcutaneous adipose tissue distribution, with low values being characteristic of women. This type of adipose tissue distribution is associated with a decreased risk of diabetes mellitus in men and in women (Krotkiewski et al., 1983; Hartz et al., 1984). In addition, the buttocks circumference has important applications in human engineering.

Literature

There are many ways in which a circumference around the hip region has been measured (Garrett & Kennedy, 1971). These can be reduced to two basic methods, plus a combination of the two. In the first, usually called "buttocks circumference," the measurement is made horizontally at the level of maximum extension of the buttocks posteriorly, as recommended. In the second, the circumference is measured horizontally at the level of the greatest lateral extension of the hips, the usual landmark being the greater trochanter. The buttocks level is recommended because it is easier to locate than the trochanteric level, because buttocks adipose tissue is related to lower limb adipose tissue (Mueller & Wohlleb, 1981), and because the buttocks circumference is generally the maximum circumference of the hip area in a horizontal plane.

Usually the trochanteric level is inferior to the level of the maximum extension of the buttocks posteriorly. Hence, when a circumference is measured at the trochanteric level, the tape tends to slip down over the buttocks. In very obese subjects, the anterior abdominal wall may sag and be included in the measurement. This is a potential problem with either of the two main methods for measurement.

Some pass the tape around both the trochanteric and buttock areas (Montagu, 1960). With this technique, the circumference is measured in an oblique plane leading to a less well-defined circumference and larger measurement errors. In the epidemiological literature, the method for the measurement of buttocks circumference is often omitted (Kalkhoff et al., 1983), or it deviates considerably from usual procedures. Some have measured this circumference at the level of the iliac crest, which is virtually the same as waist circumference (Ohlson et al., 1985).

Reliability

Little is known about the reliability of buttock circumference measurements. In a U.S. National Survey of adolescents, the technical error of measurement was 1.23 cm for intrameasurer errors and 1.38 cm for intermeasurer errors (Malina et al., 1973). Thus, the true value for an individual will be within approximately 1 cm of that recorded in most determinations. Using a slightly different measurement technique, Behnke and Wilmore (1969) found a correlation of .99 between measurements 1 day apart in young men.

Sources of Reference Data

Children

Huenemann et al., 1974
Roche & Malina, 1983

Adults

National Aeronautics and Space Administration, 1978
Clauser et al., 1970
White & Churchill, 1971

Thigh Circumference

Recommended Technique

The subject wears a bathing suit or other minimal clothing so that the appropriate landmarks can be located. Measurement of the proximal and distal thigh circumferences requires only a measuring tape. Measurement of midthigh circumference requires a grease pencil and a bench. The subject places the left foot flat on the top of the bench so that the knee is flexed to about 90°. An alternative positioning for the measurement of midthigh circumference is for the subject to sit erect with the knees flexed to about 90°. Each of the measurements is made with the subject standing, with the heels about 10 cm apart and the weight evenly distributed between both feet. The three locations are illustrated in Figures 10 and 11.

Proximal Thigh Circumference. A tape is passed horizontally around the thigh, immediately distal

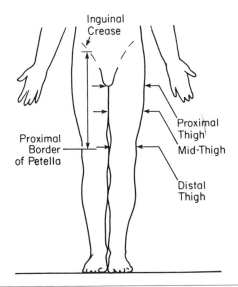

Figure 10 Anterior view of locations for thigh circumferences.

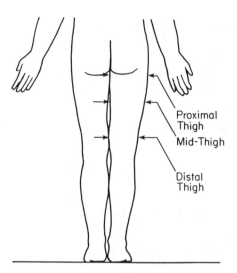

Figure 11 Posterior view of locations for thigh circumferences.

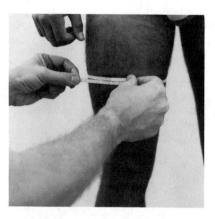

Figure 13 Measurement of midthigh circumference.

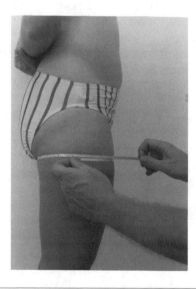

Figure 12 Measurement of proximal thigh circumference.

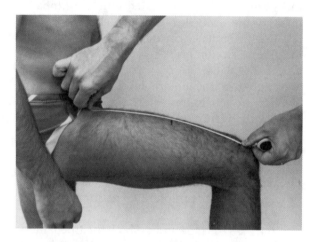

Figure 14 Locating the level for the measurement of midthigh circumference.

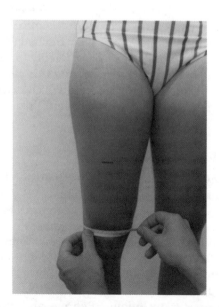

Figure 15 Measurement of distal thigh circumference.

to the gluteal furrow. This may not be the maximum circumference of the thigh (see Figure 12).

Midthigh Circumference. The measuring tape is placed horizontally around the thigh at the level of the thigh skinfold measurement, that is, midway between the midpoint of the inguinal crease and the proximal border of the patella (see Figure 13). The proximal border of the patella is marked while the subject extends the knee. The midpoint of the inguinal crease is easily located if the hips are slightly flexed. An insertion tape can be used to locate the midpoint between these points (see Figure 14).

Distal Thigh Circumference. The measuring tape is placed around the thigh just proximal to the femoral epicondyles (see Figure 15). These circumferences are recorded to the nearest 0.1 cm. Each is measured with the tape in complete contact with the skin but without compression of the soft tissues. In infants and in the elderly, these measurements can be made with the subject supine.

Purpose

The three thigh circumferences might facilitate the estimation of body density and be useful indicators of adiposity or lean body mass. Thigh circumferences, especially distal thigh circumference, are important indicators of muscle atrophy due to disease or injury, and they have applications in human engineering. It is expected that, in most studies, a selection will be made from among these measurements.

Literature

The recommended technique for the proximal thigh circumference is essentially that of MacDougall et al. (1981). Some consider that this circumference should be measured with the muscles of the thigh maximally contracted. This may decrease reliability, especially in children and the elderly. This measurement is unacceptable to some cultural groups.

Midthigh circumference has been measured midway between the greater trochanter and the proximal border of the patella. The inguinal crease has been chosen instead of the trochanter as a proximal landmark because it can be located more precisely. The recommended technique for distal thigh circumference matches that of Cameron (1978).

Rationale

The choice of technique for each of these circumferences is based on the accurate recognition of landmarks. In addition, the level recommended for the midthigh circumference matches that for the anterior thigh skinfold and thereby allows estimation of tissue areas.

Reliability

Wilmore and Behnke (1969) in a study of young men found a correlation of .99 between proximal thigh circumferences measured on two occasions, 1 day apart.

Sources of Reference Data

Children

Huenemann et al., 1974 (proximal)
Matheny & Meredith, 1947 (proximal)

Adults

National Aeronautics and Space Administration, 1978 (proximal, distal)
Clauser et al., 1972 (proximal, distal)
Hertzberg et al., 1963 (proximal, distal)

Calf Circumference

Recommended Technique

The subject sits on a table so that the leg to be measured hangs freely, or the subject stands with the feet about 20 cm apart and weight distributed equally on both feet. An inelastic tape measure is positioned horizontally around the calf and moved up and down to locate the maximum circumference in a plane perpendicular to the long axis of the calf. The zero end of the tape is placed below the measurement value. The level is marked so that a calf skinfold can be measured at the same level (see Figure 16). The maximum circumference is recorded to the nearest 0.1 cm, with the tape in contact with the whole circumference but not indenting the skin. During infancy and in the elderly, calf circumference can be measured with the subject supine and the left knee flexed to 90°.

Purpose

Calf circumference is a common measurement that can be used alone or in combination with lateral

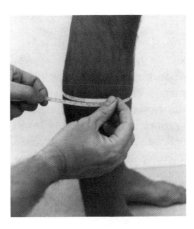

Figure 16 Measurement of calf circumference.

and/or medial calf skinfolds to provide estimates of cross-sectional muscle and adipose tissue areas of the calf. Calf circumference is important as a predictor of body composition in adults (Chumlea et al., 1984; Guo et al., 1987), and to predict body weight in the elderly (Chumlea et al., unpublished data, 1983).

Literature

Calf circumference is included in the "basic list" of anthropometric variables of Weiner and Lourie (1981). The recommended technique does not differ greatly from those reported in the literature. Calf circumference can be measured with the subject sitting on a table so that the leg hangs freely off the edge, or with the leg extended from the table, or with the subject standing with the feet separated about 20 cm and body weight distributed equally on both feet (Cameron, 1978; Malina et al., 1974; Snyder et al., 1975, 1977; Weiner & Lourie, 1981). In addition, calf circumference can be measured with the subject supine and the left knee flexed to a 90° angle (Chumlea et al., 1985); this is appropriate for infants and those who are bedfast. Comparisons have not been reported between measurements made with the subject standing and those made with the subject seated, but the differences between measurements with subjects standing and supine are very small.

Reliability

The intrameasurer technical error from Cycle III of the Health Examination Survey (6 to 11 years) was 0.87 cm, and the intermeasurer technical error was 0.34 cm (Malina et al., 1974). For children of similar age and for adults in the Fels Longitudinal Study, the intermeasurer technical error was about 0.08 cm (Chumlea & Roche, 1979). The intermeasurer technical error for elderly men and women is about 0.08 cm (Chumlea et al., 1984b). Wilmore and Behnke (1969) reported a test-retest correlation of .98 for young men measured one day apart. Intrameasurer technical errors of 0.1 to 0.5 mm and an intermeasurer technical error of 0.2 mm have been reported (Brown, 1984; Buschang, 1980; Malina, 1968; Malina & Buschang, 1984; Meleski, 1980; Zavaleta & Malina, 1982).

Sources of Reference Data

Children
Roche & Malina, 1983

Adults
Chumlea et al., 1985
Churchill et al., 1977
White & Churchill, 1971

Ankle Circumference

Recommended Technique

The subject stands barefoot on a flat elevated surface, with feet separated slightly and the weight evenly distributed between the feet. The measurer faces the side of the subject. An inelastic tape is placed around the minimum circumference of the calf, perpendicular to its long axis, just proximal to the malleoli (see Figure 17). The zero end of the tape is held below the measurement value. The tape is pulled so that it fits the ankle snugly but does not compress the underlying tissues (see Figure 18). The measurement is recorded to the nearest 0.1 cm.

Two measurers are required to measure infants and other subjects unable to stand in the appropri-

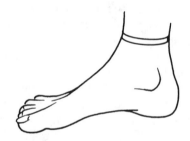

Figure 17   Level of ankle circumference measurement.

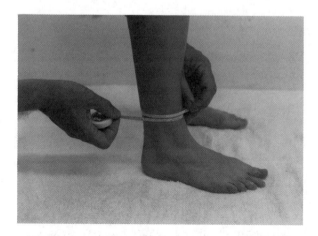

Figure 18   Measurement of ankle circumference.

ate position. The subject lies supine while one measurer elevates the leg and dorsally flexes the foot to approximately a right angle. The minimum ankle circumference is then measured as described above.

Purpose

Ankle circumference is a measure of frame size and is useful in the design of clothing, especially footwear.

Literature

Ankle circumference is measured using a tape that is sufficiently flexible to conform to the irregular shape at the level of measurement. It has been measured with the subject sitting on a table, with the feet placed in a chair high enough to form a right angle at the knee (O'Brien & Shelton, 1941). Others have measured children sitting on a table with the leg extended and relaxed (Snyder et al., 1975). The degree of dorsiflexion of the foot and support of weight by the foot are important considerations. Dorsiflexion to more than 90° is accompanied by marked contraction of the tibialis anterior and the anterior extensor muscles of the lower leg. The associated elevation of the tendons of these muscles from the surface of the ankle distorts the cross-sectional shape of the ankle and increases its circumference at the level of measurement.

Ankle circumference has been measured so that the superior border of the tape passes over the tip of the medial malleolus (O'Brien & Shelton, 1941; Randall & Baer, 1951). Ankle circumference measured in this way is not highly correlated ($r = .69$) with that measured by the recommended method (O'Brien & Shelton, 1941). The minimum circumference is recommended because reliability is known to be high, and it is the technique that has been used in studies of body composition (Wilmore & Behnke, 1969).

Reliability

Huenemann and co-workers (1974) measured ankle circumference in 2 subjects 20 times during a 4-week period. The standard deviations of replicate measurements for the 2 subjects were 0.11 and 0.12 cm for the right side and 0.12 and 0.13 cm for the left side. Wilmore and Behnke (1969) reported a test-retest correlation of .99 in young men measured on successive days.

Sources of Reference Data

Children

Huenemann et al., 1974
McCammon, 1970
Snyder et al., 1975

Adults

National Aeronautics and Space Administration, 1978
Clauser et al., 1972
White & Churchill, 1971

Arm Circumference

Recommended Technique

For this measurement the subject stands erect, with the arms hanging freely at the sides of the trunk and with the palms facing the thighs. The subject wears loose clothing without sleeves to allow total exposure of the shoulder area. If the midpoint of the upper arm has been marked for the measurement of triceps or biceps skinfolds, this should be used as the level for the measurement of arm circumference. To locate the midpoint, the subject's elbow is flexed to 90° with the palm facing superiorly. The measurer stands behind the subject and locates the lateral tip of the acromion by palpating laterally along the superior surface of the spinous process of the scapula. A small mark is made at the identified point. The most distal point on the acromial process is located and marked. A tape is placed so that is passes over these two marks, and the midpoint between them is marked (see Figure 19).

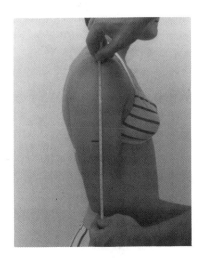

Figure 19 Location of the midpoint of the upper arm.

With the arm relaxed and the elbow extended and hanging just away from the side of the trunk and the palm facing the thigh, place the tape around the arm so that it is touching the skin, but not compressing the soft tissues. The tape is positioned perpendicular to the long axis of the arm at the marked midpoint, and the circumference is recorded to the nearest 0.1 cm (see Figure 20).

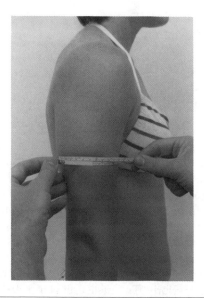

Figure 20 Measurement of arm circumference.

Purpose

Arm circumference provides an index of body energy stores and protein mass. Although it can be used as an independent measure, it is often combined with skinfold thicknesses to calculate arm-muscle circumference and the areas of arm muscle and adipose tissue (Gurney & Jelliffe, 1973; Heymsfield et al., 1984). Low values are interpreted as evidence of protein-energy malnutrition (Blackburn et al., 1977).

The recommended measurement is made with muscles relaxed. Arm circumference can be measured with the elbow flexed and the biceps contracted when there is particular interest in muscle development. This measurement is called *arm circumference-flexed*.

Literature

If possible, the subject should stand, but the arm circumference can be measured with the subject sitting erect with the back straight and the head in the Frankfort Plane.

Reliability

Bray et al. (1978) reported intermeasurer errors of selected circumferences and skinfold thicknesses in lean and obese patients. They found less variability with the circumference measurements than with skinfold thicknesses. The intermeasurer variation in obese patients after a 2-week interval was 2.1% ($\pm$ 0.10 *SEM*) for arm circumference. Hall et al. (1980) calculated the measurer error for arm circumference as 1.54 cm^2. Martorell et al. (1975) reported that in preschool children, arm circumference had a total measurement standard deviation of 0.24 cm; 56% of the total variance was due to intrameasurer variance. Intrameasurer technical errors of 0.1 to 0.4 mm and an intermeasurer technical error of 0.3 mm have been reported (Brown, 1984; Buschang, 1980; Malina, 1968; Malina & Buschang, 1984; Meleski, 1980; Zavaleta & Malina, 1982).

Sources of Reference Data

Children
Frisancho, 1974, 1981
McCammon, 1970

Adults
National Aeronautics and Space Administration, 1978
Frisancho, 1974, 1981
Bishop et al., 1981

Forearm Circumference

Recommended Technique

For the measurement of forearm circumference, the subject stands with the arms hanging downward but slightly away from the trunk, with the palms facing anteriorly (see Figure 21). The tape is placed loosely around the proximal part of the forearm, perpendicular to its long axis, and moved up and down until the level of the maximum circumference is located (see Figure 22). At this level the measurement is recorded to the nearest 0.1 cm, with the tape in contact with the skin but not compressing the soft tissues.

Purpose

Forearm circumference is used with other body measurements in some equations to predict body density from anthropometric data (Boileau et al., 1981; Jackson & Pollock, 1978; Katch & McArdle,

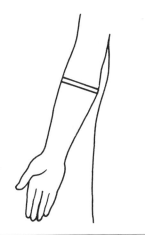

Figure 21 Diagram to illustrate the location of forearm circumference.

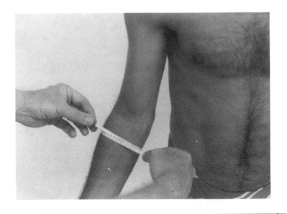

Figure 22 Measurement of forearm circumference.

1973; Pollock et al., 1975, 1976). If a forearm skinfold is measured at the same level, the cross-sectional areas of adipose tissue and of "muscle plus bone" can be estimated.

Literature

A flexible inelastic tape should be used. An insertion tape is also acceptable for this measurement. The procedures described in the literature match the recommended technique.

Reliability

Behnke and Wilmore (1969) reported a correlation of .99 between measurements 1 day apart in young men. An intrameasurer technical error of 0.2 mm was reported by Malina (1968).

Sources of Reference Data

Children

Huenemann et al., 1974

Roche & Malina, 1983

Adults

National Aeronautics and Space Administration, 1978

Wilmore & Behnke, 1969, 1980

Wrist Circumference

Recommended Technique

The measurer faces the subject who stands and flexes the arm at the elbow so that the palm is uppermost and the hand muscles relaxed (see Figure 23). An inelastic tape is placed just distal to the styloid processes of the radius and ulna, which are located by palpating with the index or middle fingers of each hand. The tape is positioned perpendicular to the long axis of the forearm and in the same plane on the anterior and posterior aspects of the wrist (see Figure 24). The tape must

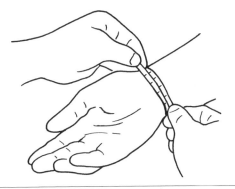

Figure 23 Positioning for the measurement of wrist circumference.

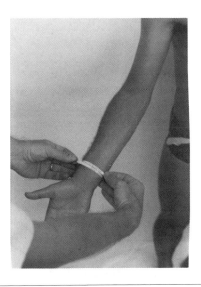

Figure 24 Measurement of wrist circumference.

be no more than 0.7 cm wide, so that it can fit into the medial and lateral depressions at this level. The measurement is made with the tape touching the skin around the whole circumference but not compressing the soft tissues. The wrist circumference is recorded to the nearest 0.1 cm.

When wrist circumference is included in a series of measurements, it is likely to be measured after another upper limb circumference, such as maximum forearm circumference. In this case, the measuring tape, still encircling the limb, is moved to the wrist region.

Purpose

Wrist circumference is a useful index of frame size because this region is relatively free from adipose tissue and muscle (Martin, 1984). Also, wrist circumference is useful as an indicator of growth, in genetic syndromology and in the modeling of body segments.

Literature

There is ambiguity in the literature over the location of the wrist circumference; hence, caution should be exercised in using reported data. In their collation of anthropometry, Garrett and Kennedy (1971) list many studies in which wrist circumference was defined as the circumference proximal to the styloid processes of the ulna and radius. For clarity, the latter measurement should be called "minimum forearm circumference."

In adults, the measurement of wrist circumference is easy because a narrow tape fits readily into the depressions present at the level of measurement. In infants, however, obtaining a satisfactory wrist circumference is impossible because the landmarks are indeterminable and the tape is generally too wide.

Reliability

Limb circumferences are highly reliable measurements; intraobserver correlations exceed .99 (Wilmore & Behnke, 1969).

Sources of Reference Data

Children

Huenemann et al., 1974
McCammon, 1970
Michael & Katch, 1968
Pieper & Jürgens, 1977

Adults

National Aeronautics and Space Administration, 1978
Clauser et al., 1972
Hertzberg et al., 1963

Chapter 5

Skinfold Thicknesses and Measurement Technique

Gail G. Harrison,

Elsworth R. Buskirk,

J.E. Lindsay Carter,

Francis E. Johnston,

Timothy G. Lohman,

Michael L. Pollock,

Alex F. Roche, and

Jack Wilmore

Skinfold thicknesses, sometimes called "fatfold" thicknesses, are actually the thicknesses of double folds of skin and subcutaneous adipose tissue at specific sites on the body. Spring-loaded or other calipers exerting standardized pressure per unit of caliper jaw surface are used, of which several types are available (see section on Equipment for details).

The utility of skinfold thicknesses is twofold. First, they provide a relatively simple and non-invasive method of estimating general fatness. The extent to which the subcutaneous adipose tissue compartment reflects total body fat varies with age as well as among individuals and populations. The predictive value of skinfold thicknesses for total body fat also varies by site, with some sites closely related to overall body composition and others relatively independent of it. Numerous equations for the prediction of body composition from anthropometric measurements have been developed (Durnin & Womersley, 1974; Jackson & Pollock, 1978; Lohman, 1981; Sloan, 1967) that make use of skinfold thicknesses as essential components.

The second major use of skinfold thicknesses is in the characterization of the distribution of sub-cutaneous adipose tissue. There is mounting evidence that not all subcutaneous adipose tissue depots are alike in terms of lability or of contribution to the health risks associated with obesity. It is particularly important to standardize site selection and location, because small differences in location can make significant differences in measurement. Because skinfold thicknesses are soft-tissue measurements, standardization of site is difficult and should always involve location in relation to unambiguous landmarks. The compressibility of both skin and adipose tissue varies with state of hydration, age, size, and individual. In general, younger individuals have more compressible skinfolds due to greater hydration of tissue. Extremes of hydration, as in edema, also effect compressibility.

The ease with which the adipose layer is separated from underlying muscle varies by site and among individuals. Very lean and very obese individuals pose special measurement problems. In general, the thicker the skinfold the more difficult it is to achieve a reproducible measure. Reliability data for skinfold measures in some populations are available for those sites that have been measured frequently, especially for those that have been included in large surveys. For some of the less commonly used sites, little or no information has been published on their inter- and intrameasurer replicability. After much deliberation, the cheek and chin were excluded from the sites for which recommended measurement techniques are described. Those interested in these sites will find details in Allen et al. (1956) and Pařízková (1977).

Skinfold Measurement Technique—General

The sites at which skinfolds are to be measured need not, in general, be marked on the subject, but this can be done, if desired. The sites must be marked in studies of intercaliper differences and when measurements of the midthigh skinfold, the triceps skinfold (at the midpoint of the upper arm), or the medial or lateral calf skinfolds (at the level of the maximum circumference of the calf) are to be combined with circumferences at the same levels to obtain estimates of cross-sectional areas.

The following description is independent of the type of caliper used and is based on the assumption that the measurer is right-handed. Palpation of the site prior to measurement helps familiarize the subject with contact in the area. The thumb and index finger of the left hand are used to elevate a double fold of skin and subcutaneous adipose tissue about 1 cm proximal to the site at which the skinfold is to be measured (Pett & Ogilvie, 1957). This separation between the fingers and the site of measurement is necessary so that pressure from the fingers does not affect the measured value. A skinfold is elevated by placing the thumb and index finger on the skin about 8 cm apart, on a line perpendicular to the long axis of the future skinfold. The thumb and index finger are drawn towards each other, and a fold is grasped firmly between them (see Figure 1).

The amount of tissue elevated must be sufficient to form a fold with approximately parallel sides. Care must be exercised so that only skin and adipose tissue are elevated. The amount of skin and adipose tissue to be elevated depends on the thickness of the subcutaneous adipose tissue at the site. The thicker the adipose tissue layer, the more separation is needed between the thumb and index finger when the measurer begins to elevate the skinfold. The errors of measurement are larger for thicker skinfolds.

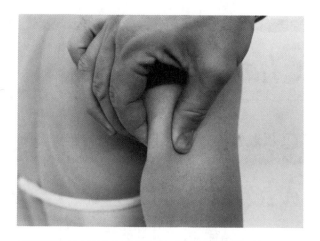

Figure 1   Position of thumb and index finger prior to grasping the fold.

The fold is raised perpendicular to the surface of the body at the measurement site (see Figure 1). The long axis of the fold is aligned as described in the instructions for each skinfold. The basic principle is that the long axis be parallel to the natural cleavage lines of the skin (Langer's lines) in the region of the measurement. The fold is kept elevated until the measurement has been completed.

The caliper is held in the right hand while a skinfold is elevated with the left hand. To make a skinfold measurement, with all except some plastic calipers, pressure is exerted to separate the caliper jaws, and the caliper is slipped over the skinfold so that the fixed arm of the caliper is positioned on one side of the skinfold. The measurement is made where the sides of the skinfold are approximately parallel (Brožek, 1961). This is approximately midway between the general surface of the body near the site and the crest of the skinfold (see Figure 2). The jaws of the caliper are placed so that the thickness of the skinfold is measured perpendicular to its long axis when the pressure on the caliper is released and the caliper jaws come towards each other. The release of pressure should be gradual to avoid discomfort.

The measurement is made about 4 seconds after the pressure is released, with the caliper and measurer positioned so that errors due to parallax are avoided (Becque et al., 1986; Ross & Marfell-Jones, 1983). If the caliper exerts force for longer than 4 seconds, a smaller measurement will be obtained because fluids will be forced out of the tissues. Timing in seconds is preferable to judgments based on the end of the rapid decrease in the measurement. A procedure has been described by Brans et al. (1974), in which skinfold thicknesses

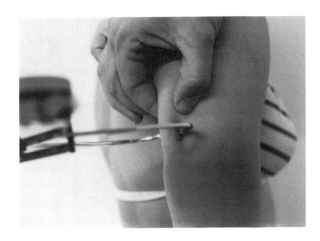

Figure 2 Measurement of skinfold thickness with caliper.

are measured at various times after application of the caliper. The changes with length of application are said to differ between premature and full-term infants.

With some plastic calipers, the jaws are apart when the calipers are not in use. When they are used, the open jaws are slipped over the skinfold and pressure is exerted, to the extent described by the manufacturer, to record a skinfold thickness. With either type of caliper, the measurement is repeated several times and the mean recorded.

With young children, it is helpful to demonstrate the caliper on the hand of the measurer and on the hand of the child, measuring total palm thickness, before beginning to measure skinfold thicknesses. The measurer must be alert to the possibility that a young child may pull away suddenly when a skinfold is being measured. If the caliper pressure is not released quickly, bruising or laceration may result.

The error due to variations in skin thickness is small, but there may be large errors due to subcutaneous edema (Keys & Brožek, 1953; Newman, 1952). In the obese, it may be impossible to elevate a skinfold with parallel sides, particularly over the abdomen. In these circumstances, a measurement is not made, unless a two-handed technique produces a satisfactory skinfold. In the two-handed technique, one measurer lifts the skinfold using two hands and another measures its thickness. This procedure gives slightly larger values (Damon, 1965). This is not recommended for general use, because of the need for a second measurer and because the reference data were not obtained in this way. In those who have lost a lot of weight, the skin is loose, and the subcutaneous

adipose tissue is soft and mobile (McCloy, 1936). Consequently, repeated measurements yield progressively lower values.

Some statistical analyses require that the data be normally distributed. Commonly the distributions of skinfold thicknesses are skewed to the right (Jackson & Pollock, 1978; Patton, 1979; Welham & Behnke, 1942). The transformation suggested by Edwards et al. (1955) usually normalize these distributions.

Subscapular Skinfold

Recommended Technique

The subscapular skinfold is picked up on a diagonal, inclined infero-laterally approximately 45° to the horizontal plane in the natural cleavage lines of the skin. The site is just inferior to the inferior angle of the scapula (see Figure 3). The sub-

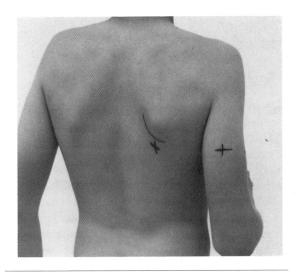

Figure 3 Landmarks for subscapular and triceps skinfolds.

ject stands comfortably erect, with the upper extremities relaxed at the sides of the body. To locate the site, the measurer palpates the scapula, running the fingers inferiorly and laterally, along its vertebral border until the inferior angle is identified. For some subjects, especially the obese, gentle placement of the subject's arm behind the back aids in identifying the site. The caliper jaws are applied 1 cm infero-lateral to the thumb and finger raising the fold, and the thickness is recorded to the nearest 0.1 cm (see Figure 4).

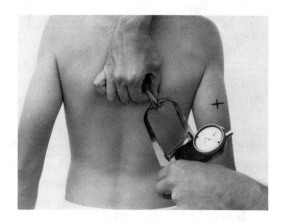

Figure 4 Measurement of subscapular skinfold.

Purpose

Subscapular skinfold thickness is a measure of subcutaneous adipose tissue and skin thickness on the posterior aspect of the torso. It is an important measure of nutritional status and, in combination with other skinfold measurements, is a useful predictor of total body fat, blood pressure, and blood lipids.

Literature

The International Biological Programme recommended the subscapular skinfold thickness as one of 21 basic measurements to be included in survey studies of growth and physique (Weiner & Lourie, 1981). Cameron (1978), citing the work of Durnin and associates (Durnin & Rahaman, 1967; Durnin & Womersley, 1974) recommended the subscapular skinfold thickness, in combination with the triceps, biceps, and suprailiac skinfold thicknesses, as the smallest number of skinfolds representative of body fat. Together with the triceps skinfold thickness, this site is used in health-related fitness tests for children.

There has been general agreement on the location of the subscapular skinfold site, although some authors recommend measuring a verticular skinfold (Cameron, 1978). A diagonal fold, in the natural cleavage of the skin, at the inferior angle of the scapula, is recommended because this makes it easier to raise a fold.

Reliability

The reproducibility of the subscapular skinfold measurement is good. Intrameasurer errors range from 0.88 (Lohman, 1981) to 1.16 mm (Wilmore & Behnke, 1969). Intermeasurer errors range from

0.88 (Sloan & Shapiro, 1972) to 1.53 mm (Johnston et al., 1972).

Sources of Reference Data

Children
Johnston et al., 1972, 1974

Adults
Durnin & Womersley, 1974
Stoudt et al., 1970

Midaxillary Skinfold

Recommended Technique

Midaxillary skinfold thickness is measured at the level of the xiphi-sternal junction, in the midaxillary line, with the skinfold horizontal (see Figure 5). The subject stands erect, except that young in-

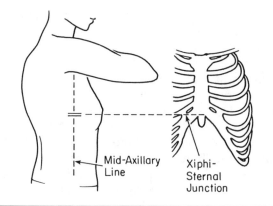

Figure 5 Illustration of the level of the xiphi-sternal junction at which the midaxillary skinfold is measured.

fants sit on the lap of the mother or caretaker. Care is taken to ensure that the subject does not flex the trunk towards the side being measured. The left arm is slightly abducted and flexed at the shoulder joint (see Figure 6). A bra can be worn while the measurement is made, but the strap may have to be undone. The measurer stands facing the side of the subject to be measured, elevates a horizontal skinfold with the left hand, and measures its thickness to the nearest 0.1 cm (see Figure 7).

Purpose

Midaxillary skinfold thickness is a guide to the total amount and the distribution of trunk subcutaneous adipose tissue. It is less highly associated than

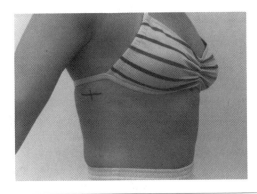

Figure 6 Subject position for midaxillary skinfold measurement.

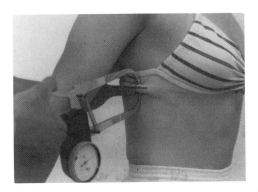

Figure 7 Measurement of midaxillary skinfold.

the subscapular skinfold thickness with the total trunk adipose tissue. It is easier to measure the midaxillary skinfold than the subscapular skinfold in bedfast individuals, and the former skinfold is less likely to be affected by edema. Also, the midaxillary skinfold is easier to measure than most other trunk skinfolds in the obese because it tends to be thinner (Johnston et al., 1974).

Literature

The literature includes few descriptions of the positioning of a subject for the measurement of the midaxillary skinfold, but the positioning in the recommended technique is in agreement with the usual practice.

Most have related the level of measurement to a bony landmark, most often the xiphoid process (Oberman et al., 1965; Pascale et al., 1956; Young, 1964). Less commonly, the measurement has been made at the level of the fifth rib (Slaughter et al., 1978; Wilmore & Behnke, 1969), or the ninth or tenth rib (Lohman et al., 1975). It has been measured midway between the nipples and the umbilicus (Johnston et al., 1974), and at the level of the nipples (Johnston et al., 1972). The latter

level usually corresponds to the fifth rib in the midaxillary line except in women.

The midaxillary skinfold, as the name implies, is measured in the midaxillary line (Johnston et al., 1974; Pascale et al., 1956; Young, 1964), but Pařiźková (1961) measured in the anterior axillary line.

The fold should be parallel to the cleavage lines of the skin at the site. These lines are nearly horizontal in the midaxillary line at the level of the xiphoid process. Nevertheless, this measurement was made across a vertical fold by Wilmore and Behnke (1969). Pascale et al. (1956) measured a vertical fold unless "the lines of Langer resulted in tension of the skinfold. Then the skinfold was taken along these lines." A fold at 45° to the horizontal was measured by Slaughter et al. (1978). Differences in thickness between horizontal and vertical folds are minimal (Chumlea & Roche, 1986).

Reliability

Using the value SD of difference/$\sqrt{2}$, the interobserver reliability was 1.47 mm in children aged 6 to 11 years in a National Center for Health Statistics Survey (Johnston et al., 1972) and was 0.36 mm for children and 0.64 mm for adults in the Fels Longitudinal Study (Chumlea & Roche, 1979). The intraobserver reliability has been reported also as the SE from a regression/$\sqrt{2}$ with values of about 1.0 mm (Wilmore & Behnke, 1969). Zavaleta and Malina (1982) reported a technical error of 0.95 mm for Mexican-American boys and of 2.08 mm for Health Examination Survey data. Lohman (1981) estimated the intrameasurer error as 1.22 mm.

Sources of Reference Data

Children
Johnston et al., 1972, 1974

Adults
Oberman et al., 1965
Young, 1964

Pectoral (Chest) Skinfold

Recommended Technique

It is recommended that the same pectoral (chest) skinfold site be used for both males and females (see Figure 8). Pectoral skinfold thickness is measured using a skinfold with its long axis directed

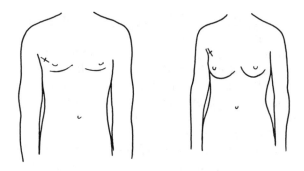

Figure 8   Illustration of location of pectoral skinfold in males and females.

to the nipple. The skinfold is picked up on the anterior axillary fold as high as possible; the thickness is measured 1 cm inferior to this (see Figure 9). The measurement is made to the nearest 0.1 cm while the subject stands with the arms hanging relaxed at the sides (see Figure 10).

For a patient confined to bed, the measurement is made while the patient is supine, with arms

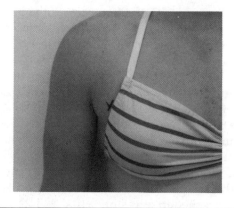

Figure 9   Location of pectoral skinfold on the anterior axillary fold.

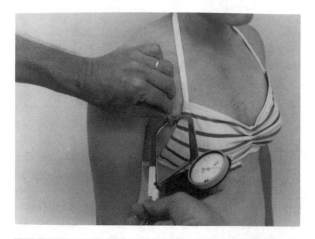

Figure 10   Measurement of the pectoral skinfold.

relaxed at the sides. For a patient confined to a wheelchair, the measurement can be made with the subject in a wheelchair with the arms relaxed at the sides.

Purpose

Pectoral skinfold thicknesses have high correlations with body density determined by hydrostatic weighing (Pollock et al., 1975, 1976). This measure has been selected by regression analysis for inclusion in equations to predict body density from anthropometric values (Pascale et al., 1956).

Literature

Pectoral skinfold thicknesses are not measured commonly. Its exclusion from many studies may result from the vague descriptions in the literature and the complexity of the measurement. Complications include the need for the removal of a T-shirt or undergarment and the need to measure away from the mammary gland in women. In most studies, a distinction is not made between the sexes in the methods for the measurement of pectoral skinfold thicknesses.

Three sites for the measurement of pectoral skinfold thicknesses are described: (a) the midpoint between the anterior axillary fold and the nipple (Pascale et al., 1956; Pollock et al., 1980); (b) juxtanipple (Pascale et al., 1956; Forsyth & Sinning, 1973); and (c) medial to the anterior axillary fold (Katch & Michael, 1968). Skěrlj et al. (1953) appear to describe a pectoral skinfold site located between those described in methods (b) and (c) above. Hertzberg et al. (1963) describe the pectoral skinfold site as juxtanipple, but their illustration shows the site as described under (a) above. The literature does not indicate the direction from the nipple of the juxtanipple skinfold site.

Skěrlj et al. (1953) describe the site as being at the axillary border of the pectoralis major muscle and state that the location is somewhat more proximal for women than for men. Pollock et al. (1984) describe the pectoral skinfold site as (a) above for males and used one third of the distance between the anterior axillary fold and the nipple for women. Depending on the size of of the mammary gland, this description for women would lead to variable site location. The main intent of describing a separate site for females was to keep the measurement away from the glandular tissue of the mammary gland.

The literature is vague, but the general impression is that most investigators measured the thickness of an oblique fold along the line of the anterior axillary fold. Hertzberg et al. (1963) measured the thickness of a vertical fold.

The same site for both males and females is desirable. Although the midpoint between the anterior axillary fold and the nipple is used most commonly for males, it is not appropriate for females. Because of the variability in the size of the mammary gland, it is difficult to use the nipple as a reference point to locate the site. Also, in most cases it would be difficult to exclude mammary tissue from measurements at the site described under (a). The recommended site allows the measurement to be made while a woman wears a two-piece bathing suit or bra.

Reliability

Intrameasurer reliability coefficients are very high, ranging from .91 to .97 (Pollock et al., 1975, 1976). The standard error of measurement *(SEM)* generally averages 1 to 2 mm. Data from 68 adults showed a correlation of .96 between trials measured on separate days with a *SEM* of 1.45 mm (Pollock, unpublished data, 1985).

Intermeasurer correlations are generally above .9, but the *SEM* may vary as much as 3 to 5 mm with inexperienced measurers, or when the site is not standardized (Lohman et al., 1984). Jackson et al. (1978) reported a correlation among measurers of .98 with a *SEM* of 2.1 mm. An intermeasurer correlation of .93 with a *SEM* of 1.7 mm has been recorded (Pollock, unpublished data, 1985).

Sources of Reference Data

Children
none reported

Adults
none reported

Abdominal Skinfold

Recommended Technique

For the measurement of abdominal skinfold thickness, the subject relaxes the abdominal wall musculature as much as possible during the procedure and breathes normally. The subject may be asked to hold his or her breath near the end of expiration if there is bothersome movement of the ab-

dominal wall with normal respiration. The subject stands erect with body weight evenly distributed on both feet. Children stand on a platform to allow the measurer appropriate access to the skinfold site.

Select a site 3 cm lateral to the midpoint of the umbilicus and 1 cm inferior to it (see Figure 11). The decision whether to measure to the left or right of the umbilicus should be consistent within a study. Raise a horizontal skinfold with the left hand and measure its thickness to the nearest 0.1 cm (see Figure 12).

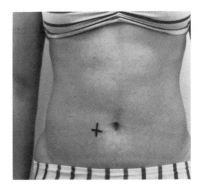

Figure 11 Location of abdominal skinfold site.

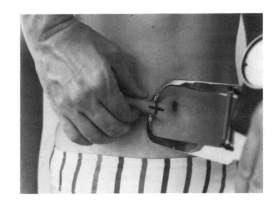

Figure 12 Measurement of abdominal skinfold.

Purpose

The abdominal skinfold is measured commonly and has been included in many studies of body fatness and in many regression equations (Lohman, 1981). Abdominal skinfold thickness changes markedly with weight reduction (Després et al., 1985). It is relatively easy to access, is relatively large, differs considerably among subjects, and is reasonably reproducible with the recommended technique.

Literature

Several locations have been used for measurement of the abdominal skinfold. These include adjacent to the umbilicus; level of the umbilicus but 5 cm to the left of it; slightly inferior to the umbilicus and 1 cm to the right of it, and a quarter of the distance between the umbilicus and the anterior superior iliac spine (Edwards, 1950; Lohman, 1981; Paṙiźková & Zdenek, 1972; Skěrlj et al., 1953; Weiner & Lourie, 1981). Most have measured horizontal fold (Behnke & Wilmore, 1974), but others have measured a vertical fold (Sinning et al., 1985; Steinkamp et al., 1965). Some subjects have a "crease" in the region of the umbilicus that precludes selection of a single site for all, and in the obese it is difficult to raise a discrete skinfold.

Reliability

Wilmore and Behnke (1969) reported a test-retest correlation of .979 for measurements made 1 day apart in young men. An intrameasurer technical error of 0.89 mm was reported by Zavaleta and Malina (1982).

Sources of Reference Data

Children
None reported

Adults
None reported

Suprailiac Skinfold

Recommended Technique

The suprailiac skinfold is measured in the midaxillary line immediately superior to the iliac crest (see Figure 13). The subject stands with feet together and in an erect position. The arms hang by the sides or, if necessary, they can be abducted slightly to improve access to the site (see Figure 14). In those unable to stand, the measurement can be made with the subject supine. An oblique skinfold is grasped just posterior to the midaxillary line following the natural cleavage lines of the skin. It is aligned inferomedially at 45° to the horizontal (see Figure 14). The caliper jaws are applied about 1 cm from the fingers holding the skinfold, and the thickness is recorded to the nearest 0.1 cm (see Figure 15).

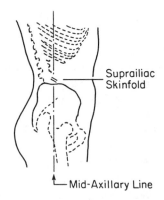

Figure 13 Diagram to illustrate the location of the suprailiac skinfold in the midaxillary line superior to the iliac crest.

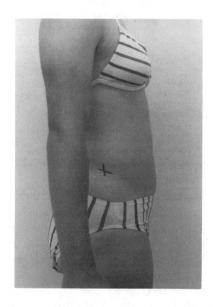

Figure 14 Subject position for measurement of the suprailiac skinfold.

Purpose

Suprailiac skinfold thicknesses are commonly used as indices of body fatness together with other skinfold thicknesses (Durnin & Womersley, 1974). Suprailiac skinfold thicknesses are useful in the study of subcutaneous adipose tissue distribution, which is important in regard to risk of disease (Lapidus et al., 1984; Larsson et al., 1984).

Literature

In most studies, the subjects stood for the measurement of suprailiac skinfold thicknesses. Considerable variation regarding the location and direction of the suprailiac skinfold occurs in the

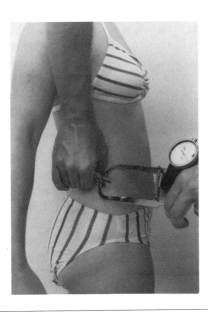

Figure 15 Measurement of the suprailiac skinfold.

literature. Thicknesses at the various locations appear highly correlated with each other and with body density (Sinning & Wilson, 1984), so that no one position appears to offer unique information. Relatively large systematic differences in thicknesses among locations emphasize the need to standardize the technique for the measurement of the suprailiac skinfold.

The selection of a site on the midaxillary line superior to the iliac crest has the advantage of being easily located in reference to anatomical landmarks. The direction of the fold parallel to the cleavage lines of the skin matches the general ap-

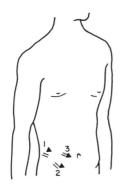

1. Standardized Suprailiac Site
2. After Pollock et al
3. After Ross and Marfell-Jones

Figure 16 Location of recommended suprailiac site in reference to other frequently measured suprailiac sites.

proach to skinfold measurement of this manual. The use of a vertical fold (Behnke & Wilmore, 1974), horizontal fold (Johnston et al., 1974), or oblique folds at more anterior locations (Pollock et al., 1975; Ross and Marfell-Jones, 1983) is common (see Figure 16).

The recommended site of measurement is very similar to the site sometimes described for the waist skinfold (Behnke & Wilmore, 1974; Brown & Jones, 1977; Skĕrlj et al., 1953). Because of this similarity, the waist skinfold procedure is not described separately.

Reliability

Wilmore and Behnke (1969) reported a test–retest correlation of .970 for values recorded 1 day apart in young men. Technical errors of 1.53 mm in children and youth (Johnston et al., 1974) and of 1.7 mm in adults (Haas & Flegal, 1981) have been reported. In each study, the errors for suprailiac skinfold thicknesses were larger than those for other skinfold sites. Intrameasurer technical errors of 0.3 to 1.0 mm have been reported by others (Buschang, 1980; Meleski, 1980; Zavaleta & Malina, 1982).

Sources of Reference Data

Children

Baker et al., 1958
Ferris et al., 1979
Johnston et al., 1974 (horizontal fold)
Montoye, 1978
Schutte, 1979
Zavaleta, 1976

Adults

Katch & Michael, 1968

Thigh Skinfold

Recommended Technique

The thigh skinfold site is located in the midline of the anterior aspect of the thigh, midway between the inguinal crease and the proximal border of the patella (see Figure 17). The subject flexes the hip to assist location of the inguinal crease. The proximal reference point is on the inguinal crease at the midpoint of the long axis of the thigh. The distal reference point (proximal border of the patella) is located while the knee of the subject is extended.

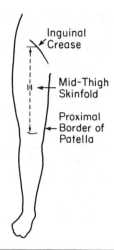

Figure 17   Location of the midthigh skinfold site.

The thickness of a vertical fold is measured while the subject stands. The body weight is shifted to the other foot while the leg on the side of the measurement is relaxed with the knee slightly flexed and the foot flat on the floor (see Figure 18). If the maintenance of balance is a problem, the subject holds the top of the measurer's shoulder, a counter top, or high-backed chair. For patients confined to a bed or wheelchair, the thigh skinfold is measured while the patient is supine. The caliper jaws are applied about 1 cm distal to the fingers holding the fold; the thickness of the fold is recorded to the nearest 0.1 cm.

Purpose

Thigh skinfold thicknesses have moderate to high correlations with body density determined by

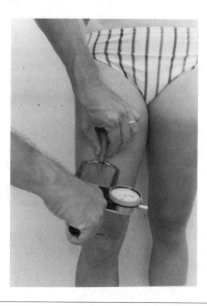

Figure 18   Measurement of midthigh skinfold.

hydrostatic weighing (Wilmore & Behnke, 1969, 1970). Thigh skinfold thickness has been selected by regression analysis as one of the skinfold measures included in equations to predict body density from anthropometric values.

Literature

A few early studies refer to both anterior and posterior thigh skinfold sites, but most refer only to the anterior site: thus, further discussion will relate to this site only.

Although description of the thigh skinfold site appears to be standardized among many studies, considerable variation can be found (Lohman et al., 1984). The most common description of the thigh skinfold site is on the anterior aspect of the thigh, midway between the hip and knee (Wilmore & Behnke, 1969; Zuti & Golding, 1973). Sloan et al. (1962) used the midpoint from the inguinal crease to the proximal margin of the patella. Others give a more general description, such as halfway down the rectus femoris muscle (Young et al., 1962).

The investigators mentioned previously described their measurements as being made with the subject in the standing position, leg relaxed. Some measure with the leg flexed 90° at the knee by placing the foot on a box. This technique is recommended by Ross and Marfell-Jones (1984). All investigators measure thigh skinfold thicknesses with a vertical fold aligned in the long axis of the thigh.

Reliability

Intrameasurer reliability coefficients are very high, ranging from .91 to .98 (Pollock et al., 1976; Wilmore & Behnke, 1969; Zuti & Golding, 1973), although the standard error of measurement (*SEM*) generally averages between 1 to 2 mm. Recent data on 68 adults showed a correlation of .985 between trials taken on separate days with a *SEM* of 1.4 mm (Pollock et al., unpublished data, 1985). Others have reported intrameasurer technical errors of 0.5 to 0.7 mm (Meleski, 1980; Zavaleta, 1976).

Intermeasurer correlations are generally above .9, but the *SEM* may be as much as 3 to 4 mm with inexperienced measurers or when the sites are not standardized (Lohman et al., 1984). Jackson et al. (1978) reported a correlation among measurers of .97 and a *SEM* of 2.4 mm for measurers of varying experience who had trained together. In an unpublished study, Pollock (1986) showed an intermeasurer correlation of .975, with a *SEM* of 2.1 mm.

Sources of Reference Data

Children
Malina & Roche, 1983
Michael & Katch, 1968
Novak et al., 1970

Adults
Shutte, 1979
Zavaleta, 1976

Suprapatellar Skinfold

Recommended Technique

The suprapatellar skinfold site is located in the midsagittal plane on the anterior aspect of the thigh, 2 cm proximal to the proximal edge of the patella (see Figure 19). A vertical fold is raised while the subject is standing. The leg on the side of the measurement is relaxed, with the body weight shifted to the other foot. The knee on the side of measurement is slightly flexed, but the sole of the corresponding foot remains in contact with the floor. If the maintenance of balance is a problem, the subject should hold onto the measurer's shoulder, a countertop, or a high-backed chair. The thickness of the fold is measured to the nearest 0.1 cm about 1 cm distal to the fingers holding the fold (see Figure 20). For patients confined to a bed or wheelchair, the suprapatellar skinfold should be measured while the patient is supine.

Purpose

Suprapatellar skinfold thicknesses have low to moderate correlations with body density, deter-

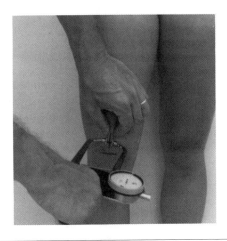

Figure 20 Measurement of suprapatellar skinfold.

mined by hydrostatic weighing or with a composite of skinfolds (r = .2 to .5; Nagamine & Suzuki, 1964; Pollock et al., 1975; Wilmore & Behnke, 1969, 1970; Young et al., 1961). Postmortem data have shown that suprapatellar skinfold thicknesses have a high correlation with total subcutaneous adipose tissue mass (r = .86; Martin, 1984). Because the subjects studied by Martin had more adipose tissue than usual, the suprapatellar skinfold thickness may be most valid with a moderately obese population.

Literature

The suprapatellar skinfold has not been used widely. Most investigators describe a vague site located over the knee or patella (Chen, 1953; Pollock et al., 1975; Wilmore & Behnke, 1969, 1970; Young et al., 1961, 1962). Skĕrlj et al. (1953), Nagamine and Suzuki (1964), and Martin (1984) have described a site proximal to the superior edge of the patella. Most do not describe the direction of the skinfold, but Wilmore and Behnke (1969, 1970) and Martin (1984) measured vertical folds.

Reliability

Intrameasurer correlations for knee skinfold thicknesses exceed .9 (Pollock et al., 1975; Wilmore & Behnke, 1969).

Sources for Reference Data

Children
None reported

Adults
None reported

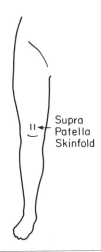

II← Supra
Patella
Skinfold

Figure 19 Location of suprapatellar skinfold site.

Medial Calf Skinfold

Recommended Technique

For the measurement of the medial calf skinfold, the subject sits with the knee on the side to be measured flexed to about 90°, with the sole of the corresponding foot on the floor. An alternative is for the subject to stand with the foot on a platform or box so that the knee and hip are flexed to about 90° (see Figure 21). The level of the maximum calf

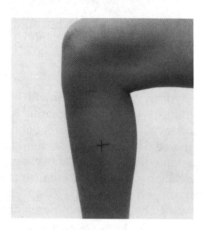

Figure 21   Foot placed on platform or box for location of medial calf skinfold site.

circumference is marked on the medial aspect of the calf (see technique for calf circumference). From a position in front of the subject, the measurer raises a skinfold parallel to the long axis of the calf on its medial aspect, when viewed from the front, at a level slightly proximal to the marked site (see Figure 22). The thickness of the fold is measured at the marked level to the nearest 0.1 cm (see Figure 23). Alternatively, the lateral calf skinfold can be measured using a corresponding procedure.

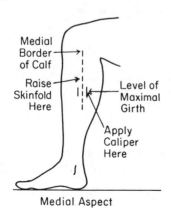

Figure 22   Medial calf skinfold site.

Figure 23   Measurement of medial calf skinfold.

Purpose

The medial and lateral calf skinfold thicknesses sample the adipose tissue in the lower leg region. These thicknesses are important in the prediction of total body fatness and in the evaluation of fat patterning.

Literature

It is important that the measurer's eyes be level with the subject's knees, or lower, so that the hands and the caliper can be placed correctly. The caliper must be horizontal, with its jaw faces parallel to the vertical axis of the fold. When the subject is seated, it may be necessary to move the other leg slightly posteriorly or laterally to allow more working room. It is necessary to elevate the limb slightly to make this measurement in recumbent subjects. Johnston et al. (1974) noted that the medial calf skinfold is technically difficult to measure and that, in about 1% of individuals, the skin and underlying tissues were "stretched" so tightly that a satisfactory fold could not be elevated. Occassionally, this measurement causes some pain or discomfort.

Medial calf skinfold thicknesses have been measured commonly (Clauser et al., 1972; De Garay et al., 1974; Heath & Carter, 1967; Johnston et al., 1974). Anterior, posterior, and lateral sites have been measured less commonly (Correnti & Zauli, 1964; De Garay et al., 1974; Škerlj et al., 1953). The lateral calf skinfold allows easier access than the medial calf skinfold, and its measurement is less likely to be painful. It is not the preferred calf site because of the paucity of reference data.

Reliability

Johnston et al. (1974) reported that the relative errors for medial calf skinfold thickness were similar to those for the suprailiac and midaxillary skinfold thicknesses. The absolute median error for all these skinfold thicknesses was 1.0 to 1.5 mm using a Lange caliper read to the nearest 0.5 mm. A test-retest correlation of .98 has been reported (Perez, 1981). In subjects with a wide range of ages, the intrameasurer correlations ranged from .94 to .99 (Carter, 1986).

Sources of Reference Data

Children

Johnston et al., 1974
Malina & Roche, 1983
Ross & Ward, 1984
Zavaleta, 1976

Adults

Clauser et al., 1972
Ross & Ward, 1984

Triceps Skinfold

Recommended Technique

The triceps skinfold is measured in the midline of the posterior aspect of the arm, over the triceps muscle, at a point midway between the lateral projection of the acromion process of the scapula and the inferior margin of the olecranon process of the ulna. The level of measurement is determined by measuring the distance between the lateral projection of the acromial process and the inferior border of the olecranon process of the ulna, using a tape measure, with the elbow flexed to 90° (see Figure 24). The tape is placed with its zero mark on the acromion and stretched along the upper arm, extending below the elbow. The midpoint

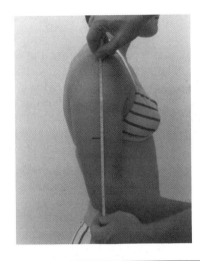

Figure 25 Marked midpoint for triceps skinfold site.

is marked on the lateral side of the arm (see Figure 25).

The subject is measured standing, except for infants and the handicapped. The skinfold is measured with the arm hanging loosely and comfortably at the subject's side (Figure 26). The caliper is held in the right hand. The measurer stands behind the subject and places the palm of his or her left hand on the subject's arm proximal to the marked level, with the thumb and index finger directed inferiorly. The triceps skinfold is picked up with the left thumb and index finger, approximately 1 cm proximal to the marked level, and the tips of the calipers are applied to the skinfold at the marked level (see Figure 26). The site of measurement must be in the midline posteriorly

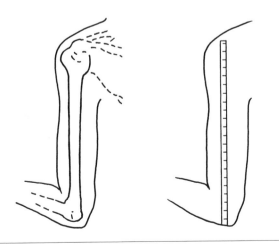

Figure 24 Location of mid-arm level for triceps skinfold.

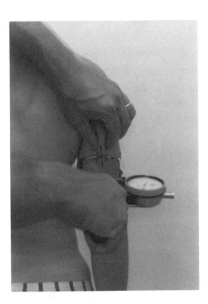

Figure 26 Measurement of triceps skinfold.

when the palm is directed anteriorly. Particular problems will be faced when measuring the obese and muscular subjects with little fat at this site. If necessary in the case of obese subjects, an assistant may pick up the fold with two hands, but this gives larger readings than if one hand is used (Damon, 1965).

Purpose

The triceps skinfold is measured more commonly than any other, partly because it is so accessible. It is closely correlated with percentage of body fat and with total body fat but is less well correlated with blood pressure than are trunk skinfolds. It is often included in studies of fat patterning.

Literature

The level of the site is marked with the arm flexed at a right angle at the elbow, and the skinfold is measured with the arm hanging loosely at the side. Positioning is not crucial, except that the subject should be relaxed and the palm directed anteriorly so that the posterior midline can be determined. Most measure subjects in a standing position, though nonambulatory patients may be measured when supine. Infants may be measured lying down, or being held on someone's lap. When supine or sitting positions are used, the recommended technique can still be applied with little modification.

Reliability

In general, measurement error increases with the age of the subject and with increasing levels of fatness. Intermeasurer technical errors vary from 0.8 to 1.89 mm (Johnston et al., 1974; Johnston & Mack, 1985). Intrameasurer technical errors vary from 0.4 to 0.8 mm (Johnston et al., 1974, 1975; Malina & Buschang, 1984; Martorell et al., 1975).

Sources of Reference Data

Children
Frisancho, 1981
Johnston et al., 1981

Adults
Frisancho, 1981
Johnston et al., 1981

Biceps Skinfold

Recommended Technique

Biceps skinfold thickness is measured as the thickness of a vertical fold raised on the anterior aspect of the arm, over the belly of the biceps muscle (see Figure 27). The skinfold is raised 1 cm superior to the line marked for the measurement of triceps

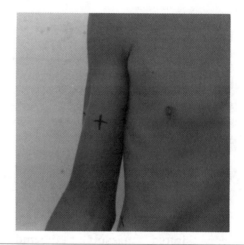

Figure 27   Location of biceps skinfold site.

skinfold thickness and arm circumference, on a vertical line joining the anterior border of the acromion and the center of the antecubital fossa (see Figure 28). The subject stands, facing the measurer, with the upper extremity relaxed at the side, and the palm directed anteriorly. The caliper jaws are applied at the marked level (see Figure 28). The thickness of the skinfold is recorded to the nearest 0.1 cm.

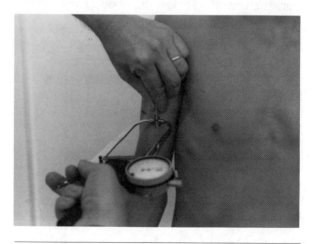

Figure 28   Measurement of biceps skinfold.

Purpose

The biceps skinfold is a measurer of subcutaneous adipose tissue and skin thickness on the anterior aspect of the arm. In combination with other skinfold measurements, it is a useful predictor of total body fat (Durnin & Womersley, 1974). Together with triceps skinfold thickness it may assist the calculation of the "muscle plus bone" cross-sectional area at this level. It can be useful in the obese, in whom many other skinfolds cannot be measured.

Literature

Biceps skinfold thickness is not measured commonly. Consequently, the site has been poorly described, and the reproducibility of measurement is not well established. The International Biological Programme included the biceps skinfold thickness as one of 10 possible skinfold thickness measurements for use in studies of growth and physique, nutritional status, and work capacity (Weiner & Lourie, 1981). More recently, Cameron (1978), based presumably on the work of Durnin and associates (Durnin & Rahaman, 1967; Durnin & Womersley, 1974), recommended biceps skinfold thickness in combination with the triceps, subscapular, and suprailiac skinfold thicknesses, as the fewest skinfold thicknesses representative of body fat; this recommendation is unlikely to be valid in both sexes and in different age groups. The biceps skinfold thickness is used mainly by workers who employ the Durnin equations to estimate percent body fat or study the obese.

Previous descriptions of the biceps skinfold have placed the site generally at the position recommended here. Subject positioning has varied between studies from sitting with the upper extremity resting supinated on the subject's thigh (Durnin & Rahaman, 1967), to standing with the upper extremity held relaxed at the side, palm facing forwards (Cameron, 1978), as is recommended. This brings the site into the anterior midline of the arm, and muscle contraction and skin tension are low.

Reliability

The standard deviation of differences for repeated measurements of biceps skinfold thicknesses by one investigator was 1.9 mm, and the standard deviation of the differences between three measurers was 1.9 mm (Edwards et al., 1955). Technical errors for intrameasurer differences are about 0.2 to 0.6 mm (Meleski, 1980; Zavaleta, 1976).

Sources of Reference Data

Children
Harsha et al., 1978
McGowan et al., 1975

Adults
Durnin & Rahaman, 1967
Durnin & Womersley, 1974
Edwards et al., 1955

Forearm Skinfold

Recommended Technique

The forearm skinfold thickness is measured with the subject standing and with shoulders and arms relaxed (see Figure 29). The arm is pendant and the palm faces the lateral aspect of the thigh. The forearm skinfold is measured at the same level as the maximum circumference of the forearm. The technique for locating the maximum circumference is described separately. The level of the maximum circumference should be marked on the skin (see Figure 30). A vertical fold is raised in the midline of the posterior aspect of the forearm between the thumb and index finger of the left hand, about 1 cm distal to the marked level. Its thickness is mea-

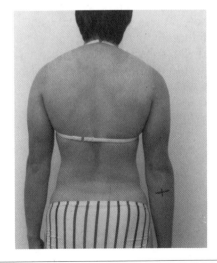

Figure 29 Subject positioning and location of forearm skinfold site on the posterior aspect of the forearm.

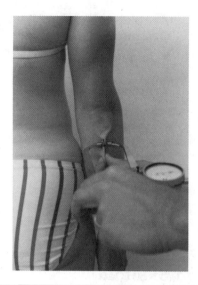

Figure 30   Measurement of forearm skinfold.

sured at the level of the marked circumference to the nearest 0.1 cm (see Figure 30).

Purpose

The forearm skinfold is measured to study adipose tissue distribution or to obtain data for a site where individual differences tend to be independent of general body fatness. This skinfold thickness is not as useful as that of the triceps skinfold for predicting total body fat or body density but may be more useful for studying individual variability in fat patterning. Albrink and Meigs (1964) claimed that forearm skinfold thickness was a good index of "inherited" fatness because it did not correlate with weight gain in adult life, nor was it closely correlated with subscapular and subcostal skinfold thicknesses. In contrast, the thicknesses of trunk skinfolds were well correlated with weight gain and with plasma triglyceride levels. More recently,

Szathmary and Holt (1983) have shown that forearm skinfold thickness is important in studies of adipose tissue patterning in relation to glucose intolerance.

Literature

The measurement is made with the arm pendant, because in this position the fold is vertical, the calipers are easier to read, and errors are less likely. Forearm skinfold thickness has been measured at the midpoint of the radius (Weiner & Lourie, 1981). The recommended site, at the level of the maximum circumference, is easier to locate. This should simplify the process and lead to fewer measuring errors. It is important that the forearm circumference and the forearm skinfold thickness be measured at the same level so that adipose tissue and muscle areas can be calculated.

The forearm skinfold has been measured on the medial (ulnar), lateral (radial), and posterior aspects of the forearm. Weiner and Lourie (1981) state the forearm skinfold "is picked up on the lateral aspect of the forearm." The posterior location is recommended, because thicknesses at this site have health-related significance (Feldman et al., 1969).

Reliability

Reliability data for forearm skinfold thicknesses are unavailable.

Sources of Reference Data

Children
Malina & Roche, 1983
Adults
None reported

References

Abraham, S., Johnson, C.L., & Najjar, M.F. (1979). *Weight by height and age for adults 18–74 years, U.S. 1971–1974, vital and health statistics* (Series 11, No. 211, Department of Health, Education, and Welfare). Washington, DC: U.S. Government Printing Office.

Albrink, M.J., & Meigs, J.W. (1964). Interrelationship between skinfold thickness, serum lipids and blood sugar in normal men. *American Journal of Clinical Nutrition*, **15**, 255–261.

Allen, T-H, Peng, M-T., Cheng, K-P., Huang, T-F., Chang, C., & Fang, H-S. (1956). Prediction of total adiposity from skinfolds and the curvilinear relationship between external and internal adiposity. *Metabolism*, **5**, 546–552.

Bailey, D. (1967). *Saskatchewan child growth and development study* (Report No. 5). Saskatoon, Canada: University of Saskatchewan.

Baker, P.T., Hunt, E.E., Jr., & Sen, T. (1958). The growth and interrelations of skinfolds and brachial tissues in man. *American Journal of Physical Anthropology*, **16**, 39–58.

Becque, M.D., Katch, V.L., & Moffatt, R.J. (1986). Time course of skin-plus-fat compression in males and females. *Human Biology*, **58**, 33–42.

Behnke, A.R. (1963). Anthropometric estimate of body size, shape, and fat content. *Postgraduate Medicine*, **34**, 190–198.

Behnke, A.R., & Wilmore, J.H. (1974). *Evaluation and regulation of body build and composition*. Englewood Cliffs, NJ: Prentice-Hall.

Bishop, C.W., Bowen, P.E., & Ritchey, S.S. (1981). Norms for nutritional assessment of American adults by upper arm anthropometry. *American Journal of Clinical Nutrition*, **34**, 2830–2839.

Blackburn, G.L., Bristrian, B.R., Maini, B.S., Schlamm, H.T., & Smith, M.F. (1977). Nutritional and metabolic assessment of the hospitalized patient. *Journal of Parenteral and Enteral Nutrition*, **1**, 11–22.

Boileau, R.A., Wilmore, J.H., Lohman, T.G., Slaughter, M.H., & River, W.F. (1981). Estimation of body density from skinfold thicknesses, body circumferences and skeletal widths in boys aged 8 to 11 years: Comparison of two samples. *Human Biology*, **53**, 575–592.

Bolton, C.B., Kenward, M., Simpson, R.E., & Turner, G.M. (1973). *An anthropometric survey of 2000 Royal Air Force Aircrew* (TR-73083). Farnborough, England: Royal Aircraft Establishment.

Borkan, G., Glynn, S., Bachman, S., Bossé, R., & Weiss, S. (1981). Relationship between cigarette smoking, chest size and body size in health-screened adult males. *Annals of Human Biology*, **8**, 153–160.

Borkan, G.A., Hults, D.E., Gerzof, S.G., Burrows, B.A., & Robbins, A.H. (1983). Relationships between computed tomography tissue areas, thicknesses and total body composition. *Annals of Human Biology*, **10**, 537–546.

Brans, Y.W., Summers, J.E., Dweck, H.S., & Cassidy, G. (1974). A noninvasive approach to body composition in the neonate: Dynamic skinfold measurement. *Pediatric Research*, **8**, 215–222.

Bray, G.A., Greenway, F.L., Molich, M.E., Dahms, W.T., Atkinson, R.L., & Hamilton, K. (1978). Use of anthropometric measures to assess weight loss. *American Journal of Clinical Nutrition*, **31**, 769–773.

Brown, K.R. (1984). *Growth, physique and age at menarche of Mexican American females ages 12 through 17 years residing in San Diego County, California*. Unpublished doctoral dissertation, University of Texas, Austin.

Brown, O.T., & Wigzell, F.W. (1964). The significance of span as a clinical measurement. In W.F. Anderson & B. Issaacs (Eds.), *Current achievements in geriatrics* (pp. 246–251). London: Cassell.

Brown, W.J., & Jones, P.R.M. (1977). The distribution of body fat in relation to habitual activity. *Annals of Human Biology*, **4**, 537–550.

Brožek, J. (1961). Body measurements, including skinfold thickness, as indicators of body composition. In J. Brožek & A. Henschel (Eds.),

Techniques for measuring body composition (proceedings of a conference, Quartermaster Research and Engineering Center; pp. 3-35). Washington, DC: National Academy of Science.

Buschang, P.H. (1980). *Growth status and rate in school children 6 to 13 years of age in a rural Zapotec-speaking community in the Valley of Oaxaca, Mexico.* Unpublished doctoral dissertation: University of Texas, Austin.

Cameron, N. (1978). The methods of auxological anthropometry. In F. Falkner & J.M. Tanner (Eds.), *Human growth: Vol. 2. Post natal growth* (pp. 35-90). New York: Plenum Press.

Cameron, N. (1984). *The measurement of human growth.* London: Coom Helm.

Carter, J.E.L. (1980). *The Heath-Carter Somatotype Method.* San Diego, CA: San Diego State University Syllabus Service.

Carter, J.E.L. (1986). Unpublished data. San Diego State University, Department of Physical Education. San Diego, CA.

Chen, K. (1953). Report on total body fat in American women estimated on the basis of specific gravity as an evaluation of individual fatness and leanness. *Journal of the Formosan Medical Association,* **52,** 271-276.

Chumlea, W.C. (1983). Unpublished data. Wright State University School of Medicine, Department of Pediatrics, Yellow Springs, OH.

Chumlea, W.C. (1985). Accuracy and reliability of a new sliding caliper. *American Journal of Physical Anthropology,* **68,** 425-427.

Chumlea, W.C., & Roche, A.F. (1979). Unpublished data. Wright State University School of Medicine, Department of Pediatrics, Yellow Springs, OH.

Chumlea, W.C., & Roche, A.F. (1986). Unpublished data. Wright State University School of Medicine, Department of Pediatrics, Yellow Springs, OH.

Chumlea, W.C., Roche, A.F., & Mukherjee, D. (1984a). *Nutrional assessment of the elderly through anthropometry.* Columbus, OH: Ross Laboratories.

Chumlea, W.C., Roche, A.F., & Rogers, E. (1984b). Replicability for anthropometry in the elderly. *Human Biology,* **56,** 329-337.

Chumlea, W.C., Roche, A.F., & Webb, P. (1984c). Body size, subcutaneous fatness and total body fat in older adults. *International Journal of Obesity,* **8,** 311-317.

Chumlea, W.C., Steinbaugh, M.L., Roche, A.F., Mukherjee, D., & Gopalaswamy, N. (1985). Nutritional anthropometric assessment in elderly persons 65 to 90 years of age. *Journal of Nutrition for the Elderly,* **4,** 39-51.

Churchill, E., Churchill, T., McConville, J.T., & White, R.M. (1977). *Anthropometry of women of the U.S. Army 1977* (Report No. 2—The basic univariate statistics. [AD-A044-806] Natick/TR-77/024). Natick, MA: United States Army.

Clarys, J.P., Martin, A.D., & Drinkwater, D. (1984). Gross tissue weights in the human body by cadaver dissection. *Human Biology,* **56,** 459-473.

Clauser, C.E., Tucker, P.E., McConville, J.T., Churchill, E., Laubach, L.L., & Reardon, J.A. (1972). *Anthropometry of Air Force women* (Report No. AMRL-TR-70-5). Dayton, OH: Aerospace Medical Research Laboratory, Aerospace Medical Division, Air Force Systems Command, Wright-Patterson Air Force Base.

Comas, J. (1960). *Manual of physical anthropology.* Springfield, IL: Charles C Thomas.

Cooke, R.W.I., Lucas, A., Yudkin, P.L.N., & Pryse-Davies, J. (1977). Head circumference as an index of brain weight in the fetus and newborn. *Early Human Development,* **1,** 145-149.

Correnti, V., & Zauli, B. (1964). *Olimpionici, 1960.* Rome: Marves.

Damon, A. (1964). Notes on anthropometric technique I. Stature against a wall and standing free. *American Journal of Physical Anthropology,* **22,** 73-77.

Damon, A. (1965). Notes on anthropometric technique: II. Skinfolds— right and left sides; held by one or two hands. *American Journal of Physical Anthropology,* **23,** 305-311.

Damon, A., Stoudt, H.W., & McFarland, R.A. (1966). *The human body in equipment design.* Cambridge, MA: Harvard University Press.

Davenport, C.B. (1921). *The medical department of the United States Army in the World War: Volume XV. Statistics: Part One. Army anthropology.* Washington, DC: U.S. Government Printing Office.

De Garay, A.L., Levine, L., & Carter, J.E.L. (1974). *Genetic and anthropological studies of Olympic athletes.* New York: Academic Press.

Demirjian, A. (1980). *Anthropometry report: Height, weight and body dimensions.* Ottawa, Canada: Ministry of National Health and Welfare.

Demirjian, A., & Jeniček, M. (1972). Latéralité corporelle des enfants Canadiens Français à Montréal. *Kinanthropologie,* **4,** 158-185.

Demirjian, A., Jeniček, M., & Dubuc, M.B. (1972). Les normes staturopondérales de l'enfant urbain Canadien français d'age scolaire. *Canadian Journal of Public Health,* **63,** 14-30.

Dequeker, J.V., Baeyens, J.P., & Claessens, J. (1969). The significance of stature as clinical measurement of aging. *Journal of the American Geriatric Society*, **17**, 169–179.

Després, J.P., Bouchard, C., Tremblay, A., Savard, R., & Marcotte, M. (1985). Effects of aerobic training on fat distribution in male subjects. *Medicine and Science in Sports and Exercise*, **17**, 113–118.

Durnin, J.V.G.A., & Rahaman, M.M. (1967). The assessment of the amount of fat in the human body from measurements of skinfold thickness. *British Journal of Nutrition*, **21**, 681–689.

Durnin, J.V.G.A., & Womersley, J. (1974). Body fat assessed from total body density and its estimation from skinfold thickness: Measurements on 481 men and women aged 16 to 72 years. *British Journal of Nutrition*, **32**, 77–97.

Edwards, D.A.W. (1950). Observations on the distribution of subcutaneous fat. *Clinical Science*, **9**, 259–270.

Edwards, D.A.W., Hammond, W.H., Healy, M.J.R, Tanner, J.M., & Whitehouse, R.H. (1955). Design and accuracy of calipers for measuring subcutaneous tissue thickness. *British Journal of Nutrition*, **9**, 133–143.

Engelbach, W. (1932). *Endocrine medicine: Vol. 1: General considerations*. Springfield, IL: Charles C Thomas.

Engstrom, F.M., Roche, A.F., & Mukherjee, D. (1981). Differences between arm span and stature in white children. *Journal of Adolescent Health Care*, **2**, 19–22.

Eveleth, P.B., & Tanner, J.M. (1976). *Worldwide variation in human growth*. Cambridge, England: Cambridge University Press.

Faulhaber, J. (1970). Anthropometry of living Indians. In R. Wauchope (Ed.), *Physical anthropology*: Vol. 9. *Handbook of middle American Indians* (pp. 82–104). Austin, TX: University of Texas Press.

Feldman, R., Sender, A.J., & Siegelaub, A.B. (1969). Difference in diabetic and non-diabetic fat distribution patterns by skinfold measurements. *Diabetes*, **18**, 478–486.

Ferris, A.G., Beal, V.A., Laus, M.J., & Hosmer, D.W. (1979). The effect of feeding on fat deposition in early infancy. *Pediatrics*, **64**, 397–401.

Forsyth, H.L., & Sinning, W.E. (1973). The anthropometric estimation of body density and lean body weight of male athletes. *Medicine and Science in Sports and Exercise*, **5**, 174–180.

Friedlander, J.S., Costa, P.T., Bossé, R., Ellis, E., Rhoads, J.G., & Stoudt, H.W. (1977). Longitudinal physique changes among healthy white veterans of Boston. *Human Biology*, **49**, 541–558.

Frisancho, A. (1974). Triceps skinfold and upper arm muscle size norms for assessment of nutritional status. *American Journal of Clinical Nutrition*, **27**, 1052–1057.

Frisancho, A.R. (1976). Growth and morphology at high altitude. In P.T. Baker & M.A. Little (Eds.), *Man in the Andes* (pp. 180–207). Stroudsburg, PA: Dowden, Hutchinson, Ross, Inc.

Frisancho, A.R. (1981). New norms of upper limb fat and muscle areas for assessment of nutritional status. *American Journal of Clinical Nutrition*, **34**, 2540–2545.

Frisancho, A.R. (1984). New standards of weight and body composition by frame size and height for assessment of nutritional status of adults and the elderly. *American Journal of Clinical Nutrition*, **40**, 808–819.

Frisancho, A.R. (1986). *Desirable anthropometric standards by frame size for the assessment of growth and nutritional status of children and adults for use with the Frameter*. Ann Arbor, MI: Health Products.

Frisancho, A.R., & Baker, P.T. (1970). Altitude and growth: A study of the patterns of physical growth of a high altitude Peruvian Quecha population. *American Journal of Physical Anthropology*, **32**, 279–292.

Frisancho, A.R., & Flegel, P.N. (1983). Elbow breadth as a measure of frame size for U.S. males and females. *American Journal of Clinical Nutrition*, **37**, 311–314.

Garrett, J.W. (1971). The adult human: Some anthropometric and biomechanical considerations. *Human Factors*, **13**, 117–131.

Garrett, J.W., & Kennedy, K.W. (1971). *A collation of anthropometry* (AMRL-TR-68-1, 2 Vols). Dayton, OH: Aerospace Medical Research Laboratory, Aerospace Medical Division, Air Force Systems Command, Wright-Patterson Air Force Base.

Gavan, J.A. (1950). The consistency of anthropometric measurements. *American Journal of Physical Anthropology*, **8**, 417–426.

Gleń, E., Glab, H., Jasicki, B., Kaczanowski, K., Karás, B., Schmager, J., Sikora, P., & Tadeusiewicz, R. (1982). Rozwój dzieci i mlodzieży w rejonie Huty Katowice na tle populacji doroslych (normy rozwojowe). *Prace Zoologiczne, Zeszyt*, **28**, 1–198.

Guo, S., Roche, A.F., Chumlea, W.C., Miles, D.S., & Pohlman, R.L. (1987). Body composition predictions from bioelectric impedance. *Human Biology*, **59**, 221–233.

Gurney, J.M., & Jelliffe, D.B. (1973). Arm anthropometry in nutritional assessment: Nomogram for rapid calculation of muscle circumference and cross-sectional muscle and fat areas. *American Journal of Clinical Nutrition, 26,* 912–915.

Haas, J.D., & Flegal, K.M. (1981). Anthropometric measurements. In G.R. Newell & N.M. Ellison (Eds.), *Progress in cancer research: Vol. 17. Nutrition and cancer: Etiology and treatement* (pp. 123–140). New York: Raven Press.

Hall, J.C., O'Quigley, J., Giles, G.R., Appleton, N., & Stocks, H. (1980). Upper limb anthropometry: The value of measurement variance studies. *American Journal of Clinical Nutrition, 33,* 1846–1851.

Hamill, P.V.V., Drizd, T.A., Johnson, C.L., Reed, R.B., & Roche, A.F. (1977). *NCHS growth curves for children birth–18 years, U.S.* (Vital and Health Statistics, Series 11, No. 165, Department of Health, Education and Welfare). Washington, DC: U.S. Government Printing Office.

Hamill, P.V.V., Drizd, T.A., Johnson, C.L., Reed, R.B., Roche, A.F., & Moore, W.M. (1979). Physical growth: National Center for Health Statistics percentiles. *American Journal of Clinical Nutrition, 32,* 607–609.

Hamill, P.V.V., Johnston, F.E., & Grams, W. (1970). *Height and weight of children* (Vital and Health Statistics, Series 11, No. 104, Department of Health, Education and Welfare). Washington, DC: U.S. Government Printing Office.

Hamill, P.V.V., Johnston, F.E., & Lemeshow, S. (1973a). *Height and weight of youths 12–17 years* (Vital and Health Statistics, Series 11, No. 124, Department of Health, Education, and Welfare). Washington, DC: U.S. Government Printing Office.

Hamill, P.V.V., Johnston, F.E., & Lemeshow, S. (1973b). *Body weight, stature, and sitting height: White and Negro youths 12–17 years, United States* (Vital and Health Statistics, Series 11, No. 126, Department of Health, Education and Welfare). Washington, DC: U.S. Government Printing Office.

Harrison, G.A., Weiner, J.S., Tanner, J.M., & Barnicot, N.A. (1964). *Human biology: An introduction to human evolution, variation and growth.* New York: Oxford University Press.

Harsha, D.W., Frericks, R.R., & Berenson, G.S. (1978). Densitometry and anthropometry of black and white children. *Human Biology, 50,* 261–280.

Hartz, A.J., Rupley, D.C., & Rimm, A.A. (1984). The association of girth measurements with disease in 32,856 women. *American Journal of Epidemiology, 119,* 71–80.

Heath, B.H., & Carter, J.E.L. (1967). A modified somatotype method. *American Journal of Physical Anthropology, 27,* 57–74.

Hendy, K.C. (1979). *Australian Tri-Service Anthropometric Survey. 1977: Part 1. Survey planning, conduct, data handling and methods of analysis* (ARL-SYS-REPORT-15). Melbourne, Australia: Aeronautical Research Laboratories.

Hertzberg, H.T.E. (1968). The Conference on Standardization of Anthropometric Technique and Terminology. *American Journal of Physical Anthropology, 28,* 1–16.

Hertzberg, H.T.E., Churchill, E., Dupertuis, C.W., White, R.M., & Damon, A. (1963). *Anthropometric survey of Turkey, Greece and Italy.* New York: Macmillan Company.

Heymsfield, S.B., Clifford, B., McManus, C., Sietz, S.B., Nixon, D.W., & Andrews, J.S. (1984). Anthropometric assessment of adult protein-energy malnutrition. In R.A. Wright & S. Heymsfield (Eds.) *Nutritional assessment* (pp. 27–82). Boston: Blackwell Scientific Publications.

Himes, J.H., & Bouchard, C. (1985). Do the new Metropolitan Life Insurance weight-height tables correctly assess body frame and body fat relationships? *American Journal of Public Health, 75,* 1076–1079.

Hrdlička, A. (1920). *Anthropometry.* Philadelphia: Wistar Institute of Anatomy and Biology.

Hrdlička, A. (1939). *Practical anthropometry.* Philadelphia: Wistar Institute of Anatomy and Biology.

Huenemann, R.L., Hampton, M.C., Behnke, A.R., Shapiro, L.R., & Mitchell, B.N. (1974). *Teenage nutrition and physique.* Springfield, IL: Charles C Thomas.

Illingworth, R.S., & Eid, E.E. (1971). The head circumference in infants and other measurements to which it may be related. *Acta Paediatrica Scandinavica, 60,* 333–337.

Jackson, A.S., & Pollock, M.L. (1976). Factor analysis and multivariate scaling of anthropometric variables for the assessment of body composition. *Medicine and Science in Sports and Exercise, 8,* 196–203.

Jackson, A.S., & Pollock, M.L. (1978). Generalized equations for predicting body density of men. *British Journal of Nutrition, 40,* 497-504.

Jackson, A.S., Pollock, M.L., & Gettman, L.R. (1978). Intertester reliability of selected skinfold and circumference measurements and percent fat estimates. *Research Quarterly for Sport and Exercise*, **49**, 546-551.

Johnson, C.L., Fulwood, R., Abraham, S., & Bryner, J.D. (1981). *Basic data on anthropometric and angular measurements of the hip and knee joints for selected age groups 1-74 years of age, United States, 1971-1975* (Vital and Health Statistics, Series 11, No. 219. U.S. Department of Health and Human Services). Washington, DC: U.S. Government Printing Office.

Johnston, F.E., Dechow, P.C., & McVean, R.B. (1975). Age changes in skinfold thickness among upper class school children of different ethnic backgrounds residing in Guatemala. *Human Biology*, **47**, 251-262.

Johnston, F.E., Hamill, P.V.V., & Lemeshow, S. (1972). *Skinfold thickness of children 6-11 years, United States, 1963-1965* (Vital and Health Statistics, Series 11, No. 120, Department of Health, Education and Welfare). Washington, DC: U.S. Government Printing Office.

Johnston, F.E., Hamill, P.V.V., & Lemeshow, S. (1974). *Skinfold thickness of youth 12-17 years, United States, 1966-1970* (Vital and Health Statistics, Series 11, No. 132, Department of Health, Education and Welfare). Washington, DC: U.S. Government Printing Office.

Johnston, F.E., & Mack, R.W. (1985). Interobserver reliability of skinfold measurements in infants and young children. *American Journal of Physical Anthropology*, **67**, 285-290.

Kalkhoff, R.R., Hartz, A.H., Rupley, D., Kissebah, A.H., & Kelber, S. (1983). Relationship of body fat distribution to blood pressure, carbohydrate tolerance, and plasma lipids in healthy obese women. *Journal of Laboratory and Clinical Medicine*, **102**, 621-627.

Kannel, W.B., & Gordon, T. (1980). Physiological and medical concomitants of obesity: The Framingham Study, *Obesity in America*, In G.A. Bray (Ed.). (pp. 125-163; Department of Health, Education and Welfare, National Institutes of Health, Publication No. 80-359). Washington DC: U.S. Government Printing Office.

Karlberg, P., Taranger, J., Engström, I., Karlberg, J., Landström, T., Lichtenstein, H., Lindström, B., & Svennberg-Redegren, I. (1976). I. Physical growth from birth to 16 years and longitudinal outcome of the study during the same age period. In J. Taranger (Ed.), *The somatic development of children in a Swedish urban community* (pp. 7-76). Göteborg, Sweden: Gotab Kungalv.

Katch, F.I., & McArdle, W.D. (1973). Prediction of body density from simple anthropometric measurements in college-age men and women. *Human Biology*, **45**, 445-454.

Katch, F.I., & Michael, E.D. (1968). Prediction of body density from skinfold and girth measurements of college females. *Journal of Applied Physiology*, **25**, 92-94.

Keys, A., & Brožek, J. (1953). Body fat in adult man. *Physiological Reviews*, **33**, 245-325.

Kondo, S., & Eto, M. (1975). Physical growth studies on Japanese-American children in comparison with native Japanese. In S.M. Horvath, S. Kondo, H. Matsui, & H. Yoshimura (Eds.), *Human adaptability: Vol. 1. Comparative studies on human adaptibility of Japanese, Causasians and Japanese-Americans* (pp. 13-45). Tokyo: University of Tokyo Press.

Krogman, W.M. (1950). A handbook of the measurement and interpretation of height and weight in the growing child. *Monographs of the Society for Research in Child Development*, **13**, Serial No. 48.

Krogman, W.M. (1970). Growth of the head, face, trunk and limbs in Philadelphia white and Negro children of elementary and high school age. *Monographs of the Society for Research in Child Development*, **35**, Serial No. 136.

Krotkiewski, M., Björntorp, P., Sjöström, L., & Smith, U. (1983). Impact of obesity on metabolism in men and women. Importance of regional adipose tissue distribution. *Journal of Clinical Investigation*, **72**, 1150–1162.

Lapidus, L., Bengtsson, C., Larsson, B., Pennert, K., Rybo, E., & Sjöström, L. (1984). Distribution of adipose tissue and risk of cardiovascular disease and death: A 12 year follow up of participants in the population study of women in Gothenburg, Sweden. *British Medical Journal*, **289**, 1261–1263.

Larsson, B., Svärdsudd, K., Welin, L., Wilhelmsen, L., Björntorp, P., & Tibblin, G. (1984). Abdominal adipose tissue distribution, obesity and risk of cardiovascular disease and death: A 13 year follow up of participants in the study of men born in 1913. *British Medical Journal*, **288**, 1401–1404.

Laubach, L.L., McConville, J.T., Churchill, E., & White, R.M. (1977). *Anthropometry of women of the U.S. Army—1977* (Report No. 1: methodology and survey plan. Technical Report TR-77/021). Natick, MA: U.S. Army Natick Research & Development Command.

Lohman, T.G. (1981). Skinfolds and body density

and their relation to body fatness: A review. *Human Biology, 53,* 181–225.

Lohman, T.G., Boileau, R.A., & Massey, B.H. (1975). Prediction of lean body mass in young boys from skinfold thickness and body weight. *Human Biology, 47,* 245–262.

Lohman, T.G., Pollock, M.L., Slaughter, M.H., Brandon, L.J., & Boileau, R.A. (1984). Methodological factors and the prediction of body fat in female athletes. *Medicine and Science in Sports and Exercise, 16,* 92–96.

MacDonald, G.A.H., Sharrard, K.A., & Taylor, M.C. (1978). *Preliminary anthropometric survey of Canadian Forces women* (Technical Report No. 78x20). Toronto, Canada: Defense and Civil Institute of Environmental Medicine.

MacDougall, J.D., Wenger, H.A., & Green, H.J. (1981). *Physiological testing of the elite athlete.* Ottawa, Canada: Canadian Association of Sport Sciences.

Malina, R.M. (1968). *Growth, maturation, and performance of Philadelphia Negro and white elementary school children.* Unpublished doctoral dissertation, University of Pennsylvania, Philadelphia.

Malina, R.M. (1986). Unpublished data. University of Texas, Department of Anthropology, Austin.

Malina, R.M., & Buschang, P.H., (1984). Anthropometric asymmetry in normal and mentally retarded males. *Annals of Human Biology, 11,* 515–531.

Malina, R.M., Hamill, P.V.V., & Lemeshow, S. (1973). *Selected body measurements of children 6–11 years, United States* (Vital and Health Statistics, Series 11, No. 123. Department of Health, Education and Welfare). Washington, DC: U.S. Government Printing Office.

Malina, R.M., Hamill, P.V.V., & Lemeshow, S. (1974). *Body dimensions and proportions, White and Negro children 6–11 years, United States* (Vital and Health Statistics, Series 11, No. 143. Department of Health, Education and Welfare). Washington, DC: U.S. Government Printing Office.

Malina, R.M., & Roche, A.F. (1983). *Manual of physical status and performance in childhood: Vol. 2. Physical performance.* New York: Plenum Publishing Corporation.

Martin, A.D. (1984). *An anatomical basis for assessing human body composition: Evidence from 25 dissections.* Unpublished doctoral dissertation, Simon Fraser University, Burnaby, British Columbia, Canada.

Martin, A.D. (1986). Unpublished data. Simon Fraser University, Burnaby, British Columbia, Canada.

Martin, R., & Saller, K. (1959). *Lehrbuch der Anthropologie.* Stuttgart, West Germany: Fischer.

Martin, W.E. (1954). *The functional body measurements of school age children: A handbook for manufacturers, design engineers, architects, and school officials for use in planning school furniture, equipment, and buildings.* Chicago: National School Service Institute.

Martin, W.E. (1955). *Children's body measurements for planning and equipping schools* (Special Public. No. 4. Office of Education, Department of Health, Education and Welfare). Washington, DC: U.S. Government Printing Office.

Martorell, R., Habicht, J-P., Yarbrough, C., Guzmán, G., & Klein, R.E. (1975). The identification and evaluation of measurement variability in the anthropometry of preschool children. *American Journal of Physical Anthropology, 43,* 347–352.

Matheny, W.D., & Meredith, H.V. (1947). Mean body size of Minnesota schoolboys of Finnish and Italian ancestry. *American Journal of Physical Anthropology, 5,* 343–355.

Matiegka, J. (1921). The testing of physical efficiency. *American Journal of Physical Anthropology, 4,* 223–230.

McCammon, R. (1970). *Human growth and development.* Springfield, IL: Charles C Thomas.

McCloy, C.H. (1936). *Appraising physical status. The selection of measurements* (Vol. 12). University of Iowa Studies in Child Welfare, Iowa City, IA.

McConville, J.T., Churchill, E., Churchill, T., & White, R.M. (1977). *Anthropometry of women of the U.S. Army—1977* (Report No. 5, Comparative Data for U.S. Army Men. TR-7-029). Natick, MA: United States Army.

McGowan, A., Jordan, M., & MacGregor, J. (1975). Skinfold thickness in neonates. *Biology of the Neonate, 23,* 66–84.

McPherson, J.R., Lancaster, D.R., & Carroll, J.C. (1978). Stature change with aging in black Americans. *Journal of Gerontology, 33,* 20–25.

Meleski, B.W. (1980). *Growth, maturity, body composition and familial characteristics of competitive swimmers 8 to 18 years of age.* Unpublished doctoral dissertation, University of Texas, Austin.

Meredith, H. (1970). Body size of contemporary groups of one-year-old infants studied in different parts of the world. *Child Development, 41,* 551–600.

Meredith, H.V., & Spurgeon, J.H. (1980). Somatic comparisons at age 9 years for South Carolina white girls and girls of other ethnic groups. *Human Biology, 52,* 401–411.

Michael, E.D., Jr., & Katch, F.I. (1968). Prediction

of body density from skinfold and girth. Measurements of 17 year-old boys. *Journal of Applied Physiology*, **25**, 747–750.

Montagu, M.F.A. (1960). *A handbook of anthropometry*. Springfield, IL: Charles C Thomas.

Montoye, H.J. (1978). *An introduction to measurement in physical education*. Boston: Allyn and Bacon.

Moore, W.M., & Roche, A.F. (1983). *Pediatric anthropometry* (2nd ed.). Columbus, OH: Ross Laboratories.

Morris, A., Wilmore, J., Atwater, A., & Williams, J. (1980). Anthropometric measurements of 3–4 and 5–6 year old boys and girls. *Growth*, **40**, 253–267.

Mueller, W.H., & Wohlleb, J.C. (1981). Anatomical distribution of subcutaneous fat and its description by multivariate methods: How valid are principle components? *American Journal of Physical Anthropology*, **54**, 25–35.

Nagamine, S., & Suzuki, S. (1964). Anthropometry and human composition of Japanese young men and women. *Human Biology*, **36**, 8–15.

National Aeronautics and Space Administration. (1978). *Anthropometric source book vol. I: Anthropometry for designers: Vol. II: A handbook of anthropometric data* (No. 1024). Houston, TX: Lyndon B. Johnson Space Center.

Nellhaus, G. (1968). Head circumference from birth to eighteen years: Practical composite international and interracial graphs. *Pediatrics*, **41**, 106–114.

Newman, R.W. (1952). *The assessment of military personnel by 1912 height-weight standards* (Report No. 194). Natick, MA: Environmental Protection Branch, Office of the Quartermaster General, U.S. Army.

Novak, L.P., Hamamoto, K., Orvis, A.L., & Burke, E.C. (1970). Total body potassium in infants. Determination by whole-body counting of radioactive potassium (^{40}K). *American Journal of Diseases of Children.*, **119**, 419–423.

Oberman, A., Lane, N.E., Mitchell, R.E., & Graybiel, A. (1965). *The thousand aviator study: Distributions and intercorrelations of selected variables* (Monograph 12). Pensacola, FL: U.S. Naval Aerospace Medical Institute.

O'Brien, R., & Shelton, W.C. (1941). *Women's measurements for garment and pattern construction* (Public. No. 454, Department of Agriculture). Washington, DC: U.S. Government Printing Office.

Ohlson, L.O., Larsson, B., Svärdsudd, K., Welin, L., Eriksson, H., Wilhelmsen, L., Björntorp, P., & Tibblin, G. (1985). The influence of body fat distribution on the incidence of diabetes mellitus. *Diabetes*, **34**, 1055–1058.

Olivier, G. (1969). *Practical anthropology*. Springfield, IL: Charles C Thomas.

Osborne, R., & De George, F. (1959). *Genetic bases of morphological variation*. Cambridge, MA: Harvard University Press.

Pařížková, J. (1961). Total body fat and skinfold thickness in children. *Metabolism*, **10**, 794-807.

Pařížková, J. (1977). *Body fat and physical fitness*. The Hague, The Netherlands: Martinus Nijhoff.

Pařížková, J., & Zdenek, R. (1972). The assessment of depot fat in children from skinfold thickness measurements by Holtain (Tanner/Whitehouse caliper). *Human Biology*, **44**, 613-620.

Parnell, W.R. (1954). Somatotyping by physical anthropometry. *American Journal of Physical Anthropology*, **12**, 209-239.

Pascale, L.R., Grossman, M.I., Sloane, H.S., & Frankel, T. (1956). Correlations between thickness of skinfolds and body density in 88 soldiers. *Human Biology*, **28**, 165-176.

Patton, J.L. (1979). *A study of distributional normality of skinfold measurements*. Unpublished master's thesis, University of Washington, Seattle.

Perez, B.M. (1981). *Los atletas venezolanos. Su tipo fisico*. Caracas, Venezuela: Universidad Central de Venezuela.

Pett, L.B., & Ogilvie, G.F. (1957). The report on Canadian average weights, heights and skinfolds. *Canadian Bulletin of Nutrition*, **5**, 1–81.

Pieper, U., & Jürgens, H.W. (1977). *Anthropometriche Untersuchungen zv Bav und Funktion des Kindlichen Körpers*. Bundensanstaldt für Arbeitsschutz und Unfallforsehung, Dortmund. Furschungbericht No. 178.

Pollock, M.L. (1986). Unpublished data. University of Florida, Department of Exercise Science, Gainesville.

Pollock, M.L., Hickman, T., Kendrick, Z., Jackson, A., Linnerud, A.C., & Dawson, G. (1976). Prediction of body density in young and middle-aged men. *Journal of Applied Physiology*, **40**, 300-304.

Pollock, M.L., & Jackson, A. (1984). Research progress in validation of clinical methods of assessing body composition. *Medicine and Science in Sports and Exercise*, **16**, 606-613.

Pollock, M.L., Laughridge, E.E., Coleman, B., Linnerud, A.C., & Jackson, A. (1975). Prediction of body density in young and middle-aged women. *Journal of Applied Physiology,* **38,** 745-749.

Pollock, M.L., Schmidt, D.H., & Jackson, A.S. (1980). Measurement of cardio-respiratory fitness and body composition in the clinical setting. *Comprehensive Therapy,* **6,** 12-27.

Pollock, M.L., Wilmore, J.H., & Fox, S.M. (1984). *Exercise in health and disease. Evaluation and prescription for prevention and rehabilitation.* Philadelphia: W.B. Saunders.

Randall, F.E., & Baer, M.J. (1951). *Survey of body sizing of army personnel, male and female: 1. Methodology.* (Report No. 122). Lawrence, MA: US Quartermaster Climatic Research Laboratory.

Robinow, M., & Chumlea, W.C. (1982). Standards for limb bone length ratios in children. *Radiology,* **143,** 433-436.

Roche, A.F., & Chumlea, W.C. (1985). Unpublished data. Wright State University School of Medicine, Department of Pediatrics, Yellow Springs, OH.

Roche, A.F., & Davila, G.H. (1974). Differences between recumbent length and stature within individuals. *Growth,* **38,** 313-320.

Roche, A.F., & Himes, J.H. (1980). Incremental growth charts. *American Journal of Clinical Nutrition,* **33,** 2041-2052.

Roche, A.F., & Malina, R.M. (1983). *Manual of physical status and performance in childhood: Vol. 1. Physical status.* New York: Plenum.

Roche, A.F., Mukherjee, D., Guo, S., & Moore, W.M. (1987). Head circumference reference data: Birth to 18 years. *Pediatrics,* **79,** 706-712.

Roebuck, J.A., Kroemer, K.H.E., & Thomson, W.G. (1975). *Engineering anthropometry methods.* New York: Wiley.

Ross, W.D., Brown, S.R., Hebbelinck, M., & Falkner, R.A. (1978). Kinanthropometry terminology and landmarks. In R.J. Shepard & H. Lavallee (Eds.), *Physical fitness assessment* (pp. 44-50). Springfield, IL: Charles C Thomas.

Ross, W.D., & Marfell-Jones, M.J. (1982). Kinanthropometry. In J.D. MacDougall, H.A. Wenger, & H.J. Green (Eds.), *Physiological testing of the elite athlete* (pp. 75-115). Ottawa, Canada: Canadian Association of Sport Sciences.

Ross, W.D., & Ward, R. (1984). *The O-Scale System.* Surrey, British Columbia, Canada: Rosscraft.

Rossman, I. (1979). The anatomy of aging. In I. Rossman (Ed.), *Clinical geriatrics* (2nd ed., pp. 3-22). Philadelphia: J.B. Lippincott.

Schutte, J.E. (1979). *Growth and body composition of lower and middle income adolescent black males.*

Unpublished doctoral dissertation, Southern Methodist University, Dallas, TX.

Simmons, K. (1944). The Brush Foundation Study of Child Growth and Development: II. Physical growth and development. *Monographs of the Society for Research in Child Development,* **9,** No. 1, Serial No. 37.

Singh, I., & Bhasin, M. (1968). *Anthropometry.* Delhi, India: Bharti Bhawan.

Sinning, W.E., Dolny, D.G., Little, K.D., Cunningham, L.N., Racaniello, A., Sicnolfi, S.F., & Sholes, J.L. (1985). Validity of "generalized" equations for body composition analysis in male athletes. *Medicine and Science in Sports and Exercise,* **17,** 124-130.

Sinning, W.E., & Wilson, J.R. (1984). Validity of "generalized" equations for body composition analysis in women athletes. *Research Quarterly for Exercise and Sport,* **55,** 153-160.

Skĕrlj, B., Brožek, J., & Hunt, E.E., Jr. (1953). Subcutaneous fat and age changes in body build and body form in women. *American Journal of Physical Anthropology,* **11,** 577-600.

Slaughter, M.H., Lohman, T.G., & Boileau, R.A. (1978). Relationship of anthropometric dimensions to lean body mass in children. *Annals of Human Biology,* **5,** 469-482.

Sloan, A.W. (1967). Estimation of body fat in young men. *Journal of Applied Physiology,* **23,** 311-315.

Sloan, A.W., Burt, J.J., & Blyth, C.S. (1962). Estimation of body fat in young women. *Journal of Applied Physiology,* **17,** 967-970.

Sloan, A.W., & Shapiro, M. (1972). A comparison of skinfold measurements with three standard calipers. *Human Biology,* **44,** 29-36.

Smith, D.W. (1976). *Recognizable patterns of human malformation, genetic, embryologic and clinical aspects* (2nd ed.). Philadelphia: W.B. Saunders.

Snow, C.C., Reynolds, H.M., & Allgood, M.A. (1975). *Anthropometry of airline stewardesses* (Report No. FAA-AM-75-2). Oklahoma City, OK: Office of Aviation Medicine, Federal Aviation Administration, Department of Transportation.

Snyder, R.G., Schneider, L.W., Owings, C.L., Reynolds, H.M., Golomb, D.H., & Schork, M.A. (1977). *Anthropometry of infants, children and youths to age 18 for product safety design* (Publication 77-177). Ann Arbor, University of Michigan, Highway Safety Research Institute.

Snyder, R.G., Spencer, M.L., Owings, C.L., & Schneider, L.W. (1975). *Anthropometry of U.S. infants and children* (Publication SP-394, Paper

No. 750423). Warrendale, PA: Society of Automotive Engineers.

Steel, M.F. & Mattox, J.W. (1987). Unpublished raw data. Department of Food, Nutrition, and Institute Management, East Carolina University, Greenville, NC.

Steinkamp, R.C., Cohen, N.L., Siri, W.E., Sargent, T.W., & Walsh, H.E. (1965). Measures of body fat and related factors in normal adults: I. Introduction and methodology. *Journal of Chronic Diseases, 18,* 1279–1289.

Stewart, L.E. (1985). *Anthropometric survey of Canadian Forces aircrew* (Tech. Rep. No. 85-12-01). Toronto, Canada: Human Elements Incorporated.

Stolz, H.R., & Stolz, L.M. (1951). *Somatic development of adolescent boys.* New York: Macmillan.

Stoudt, H., Damon, A., & McFarland, R. (1970). *Skinfolds, body girths, biacromial diameter and selected anthropometric indices of adults, United States, 1960–1962* (Vital and Health Statistics, Series 11, No 35. U.S. Department of Health, Education and Welfare). Washington, DC: U.S. Government Printing Office.

Stoudt, H., Damon, A., McFarland, R., & Roberts, J. (1965). *Weight, height and selected body dimensions of adults, United States, 1960–1962* (Vital and Health Statistics, Series 11, No. 8. U.S. Department of Health, Education and Welfare). Washington, DC: U.S. Government Printing Office.

Sumner, E.E., & Whitacre, J. (1931). Some factors affecting accuracy in the collection of data on the growth of weight in school children. *Journal of Nutrition, 4,* 15–33.

Szathmary, E.J.E., & Holt, N. (1983). Hyperglycemia in Dogrib Indians of the Northwest Territories, Canada: Association with age and a centripetal distribution of body fat. *Human Biology, 55,* 493-515.

Tuddenham, R.D., & Snyder, M.M. (1954). *Physical growth of California boys and girls from birth to eighteen years.* Berkeley, CA: University of California Press.

Valk, I.M. (1971). Accurate measurement of the length of the ulna and its application in growth measurement. *Growth, 35,* 297–310.

Valk, I.M. (1972). Ulnar length and growth in twins with a simplified technique for ulnar measurement using a condylograph. *Growth, 36,* 291–309.

Valk, I.M., Langhout Chabloz, A.M.E., & Gilst, W. van. (1983b). Intradaily variation of the human lower leg length and short term growth—A longitudinal study in fourteen children. *Growth, 47,* 397–402.

Valk, I.M., Langhout Chabloz, A.M.E., Smals, A.G.H., Kloppenborg, P.W.C., Cassorla, F.G., & Schutte, E.A.S.T. (1983a). Accurate measurements of the lower leg length and the ulnar length and its application in short term growth measurement. *Growth, 47,* 53–66.

Van Wieringen, J.C., Wafelbakker, F., Verbrugge, H.P., & de Haas, J.H. (1971). *Growth diagrams 1965 Netherlands.* Groningen, The Netherlands: Wolters-Noordhoff Publishing.

Verghese, K.P., Scott, R.B., Teixeira, G., & Ferguson, A.D. (1969). Studies in growth and development: XII. Physical growth of North American Negro children. *Pediatrics, 44,* 243–247.

von Döbeln, W. (1964). Determination of body constituents. In G. Blix (Ed.), *Occurrences, causes and prevention of overnutrition* (pp. 103–106). Uppsala, Sweden: Almquist and Wiksell.

Weiner, J.S., & Lourie, J.A. (1981). *Practical human biology.* New York: Academic Press.

Welham, W.C., & Behnke, A.R. (1942). The specific gravity of healthy men. *Journal of the American Medical Association, 118,* 498–501.

Weltman, A., & Katch, V. (1975). Preferential use of casing (girth) measures for estimating body volume and density. *Journal of Applied Physiology, 38,* 560–563.

White, R., & Churchill, E. (1971). *The body size of soldiers.* (TR72-51-CE). Natick, MA: U.S. Army Natick Laboratories.

Whitehouse, R.H., Tanner, J.M., & Healy, M.J.R. (1974). Diurnal variation in stature and sitting-height in 12–14 year old boys. *Annals of Human Biology, 1,* 103–106.

Wilder, H.H. (1920). *A laboratory manual of anthropometry.* Philadelphia: Blakiston's Son and Company.

Wilmore, J.H., & Behnke, A.R. (1969). An anthropometric estimation of body density and lean body weight in young men. *Journal of Applied Physiology, 27,* 25–31.

Wilmore, J.H., & Behnke, A.R. (1970). An anthropometric estimation of body density and lean body weight in young women. *American Journal of Clinical Nutrition, 23,* 267–274.

Wilson, R.S. (1979). Twin growth: Initial deficit, recovery, and trends in concordance from birth to nine years. *Annals of Human Biology, 6,* 205–220.

Wolański, N., Niemiec, S., & Pyżuk, M. (1975). *Anthropometria Inzynieryjna.* Warsaw, Poland: Ksiazka i Wiedza.

Young, C.M. (1964). Predicting specific gravity and

body fatness in older women. *Journal of the American Dietetic Association*, **45**, 333–338.

Young, C.M., Martin, M., Chihan, M., McCarthy, M., Manniello, M., Harmuth, E., & Fryer, J. (1961). Body composition of young women. *Journal of the American Dietetic Association* **38**, 332–340.

Young, C.M., Martin, M., Tensuan, R., & Blondin, J. (1962). Predicting specific gravity and body fatness in young women. *Journal of the American Dietetic Association*, **40**, 102–107.

Zavaleta, A.N. (1976). *Densitometric estimates of body composition in Mexican Americans*. Unpublished doctoral dissertation, University of Texas, Austin.

Zavaleta, A.N., & Malina, R.M. (1982). Growth and body composition of Mexican-American boys 9 through 14 years of age. *American Journal of Physical Anthropology*, **57**, 261-271.

Zuti, W.B., & Golding, L.A. (1973). Equations for estimating percent body fat and body density in active adults. *Medicine and Science in Sports and Exercise*, **5**, 262–266.

Appendix

List of Equipment and Suppliers

Equipment

Stadiometers, Scales, Miscellaneous

Holtain, Ltd.
Pfister Import-Export, Inc.

Harpenden Stadiometer
Portable
Pocket
    Raven Equipment, Ltd.
    Stanley-Mabo, Ltd.
    CMS Weighing Equipment, Ltd.

Holtain Electronic Stadiometer
    Holtain, Ltd.

Blueprints for the production of stadiometers
    Center for Disease Control

Anthropometers

Harpenden Anthropometer
    Pfister Import-Export, Inc.
    Holtain, Ltd.

GPM (Martin type) Anthropometer
    Pfister Import-Export, Inc.
    Owl Instruments, Inc.

Recumbent Length/Sitting Height Measurement Equipment

Infant Heightometer
    Hultafors AB
    Infanitometer Instrumentation Corporation

Baby Length Measurer
    Appropriate Health Resources and Technologies
        Action Group (AHRTAC)

Harpenden Sitting Height Table
Harpenden Neonatometer

Harpenden Infantometer
Holtain Electronic Infantometer
Harpenden Supine Measuring Table
    Holtain, Ltd.

Weighing Scales

Designs for making scales locally
    Hesperian Foundation
    AHRTAC
    Continental Scale Corporation
    CMS Weighing Equipment, Ltd.
    Detecto Scales, Inc.
    Salter International Measurement, Ltd.
    Marsden Weighing Machine Group, Ltd.

Dial scales for field work
    CMS Weighing Equipment, Ltd.
        (Model 235-PBW)
    Salter International Measurement, Ltd.
        (Model 235)
    John Chatillon and Sons
    Rasmussen, Webb & Company

Electronic Scales:
    Toledo scale
        Infant Scale: "Baby weight"
        Model 1365
        Children/Adult Scales: "Weight plate"
        a. Pediatric 12" x 12" plate, 150 lb. capacity
            Model 2300
        b. Adult 18" x 18" plate, 300 lb. capacity
            Model 2300

Calipers

Sliding Calipers (Large)
    Mediform sliding caliper (80 mm)

Sliding Calipers (Small)
Sliding Caliper (Martin Type)

Sliding Caliper (Holtain, 14 cm)
Sliding Caliper (Poech Type)
  Pfister Import-Export, Inc.

Spreading Calipers
Spreading Caliper (Martin Type) 0–300 mm
Spreading Caliper (Martin Type) 0–600 mm
  Pfister Import-Export, Inc.

Anthropometric Tapes

Disposable paper tape for newly-born infants
  Medline Industries

Retractable, Fiberglass Measuring Tape
  Buffalo Medical Specialties
  (available through local distributors)
  e.g. Burlingame Surgical Supply Co.

Retractable, Flexible Steel Tape
  Keuffel and Esser Co. (200 cm No. 860358)
  (available through local distributors)
  e.g. San Diego Blueprint

Scoville-Dritz Fiberglass Measuring Tape
  (available through local distributors)
  e.g. Quinton Instruments

Inser-Tape, Ross Insertion Tape
  Ross Laboratories

Linen Measuring Tape
  Pfister Import-Export, Inc.

Gulick Measuring Tape
  Country Technology, Inc.

Anthropometric Tape Measure (150 cm No. 67022)
  Country Technology, Inc.

Skinfold Calipers

Harpenden Skinfold Calipers
  H.E. Morse Co.
  British Indicators, Ltd.

Lange Skinfold Calipers
  Cambridge Scientific Industries
  Pfister Import-Export, Inc.
  J.A. Preston Corp.
  Owl Industries, Ltd.

Lafayette Skinfold Calipers
  Lafayette Instrument Co.

Slim Guide Skinfold Caliper
  Creative Health Products
  Rosscraft, Ltd.
  Country Technology, Inc.

Skyndex Electronic Body Fat Calculator—
  System I and II
  Cramer Products
  Human Performance Systems, Inc.

Fat-O-Meter Skinfold Caliper
  Health & Education Services
  Miller & Sons Assoc., Inc.

Fat Control Caliper
  Fat Control, Inc.

Adipometer Skinfold Caliper
  Ross Laboratories

McGaw Skinfold Caliper
  McGaw Laboratories

Holtain/Tanner/Whitehouse Skinfold Caliper
  and Holtain Slim-Kit Caliper
  Holtain, Ltd.
  Pfister Import-Export, Inc.

Miscellaneous by Supplier

Pfister Import-Export, Inc.
  Harpenden Vernier Caliper
  Survey Set—contains: Anthropometer, Skinfold
    Caliper, 2 Steel Tapes, Somatotype Turntable,
    Manual
  Base Plate for Anthropometer
  Curved Cross Bars
  Small Instrument Bag (Martin Type) contains:
    Sliding Caliper, Spreading Caliper, Steel
    Measuring Tape
  Large Instrument Bag (Martin Type) contains:
    Anthropometer, Recurved Measuring
    Branches, Sliding Caliper, Spreading
    Caliper, Steel Measuring Tape

Addresses of Suppliers

AHRTAC
85 Marlebone High Street
London, W1M 3DE, UK

British Indicators, Ltd.
Sutton Road
St. Albans, Herts., UK

Burlingame Surgical Supply Co.
1515 4th Avenue
San Diego, CA 92101
Phone: (619) 231-0187

Cambridge Scientific Industries
P.O. Box 265
Cambridge, MD 21613
Phone: (800) 638-9566
(301) 228-5111

Center for Disease Control
Division of Nutrition
1600 Clifton Road
Atlanta, GA 30333

CMS Weighing Equipment, Ltd.
18 Camden High Street
London, NWI OJH, UK

Continental Scale Corporation
7400 West 100th Place
Bridgeview, IL 60455
Phone: (312) 598-9100

Country Technology, Inc.
P.O. Box 87
Gays Mills, WI 54631
Phone: (608) 735-4718

Cramer Products
P.O. Box 1001
Gardner, KS 66030
Phone: (913) 884-7511

Creative Health Products
5148 Saddle Ridge Road
Plymouth, MI 48170
Phone: (313) 453-5309
(313) 455-0177

Detecto Scales, Inc.
Detecto International
103-00 Foster Avenue
Brooklyn, NY 11236

Fat Control, Inc.
P.O. Box 10117
Towson, MD 21204

H.E. Morse Co.
455 Douglas Avenue
Holland, MI 49423
Phone (616) 396-4604

Health & Education Services
Division of Novel Products
80 Fairbanks, Unit 12
Addison, IL 60101
Phone: (312) 628-1787

Hesperian Foundation
P.O. Box 1692
Palo Alto, CA 94302

Holtain, Ltd.
Crosswell, Crymmych, Dyfed
Wales

Hultafors AB
S-517 01 Bollebygd
Sweden

Human Performance Systems, Inc.
P.O. Drawer 1324
Fayetteville, AR 72701
Phone: (501) 521-3180

Infanitometer Instrumentation Corporation
Elimeankatv-22-24
SF-00510
Helsinki, No. 51
Finland

J.A. Preston Corp.
71 Fifth Avenue
New York, NY 10003

John Chatillon and Sons
83-30 Kew Gardens Road
Kew Gardens, NY 11415

Lafayette Instrument Co.
P.O. Box 5729
Lafayette, IN 47903
Phone: (317) 423-1505

McGaw Laboratories
Division of American Hospital Supply
Irvine, CA 92714

Marsden Weighing Machine Group, Ltd.
388 Harrow Road
London WG-2HV, UK

Mediform sliding caliper
5150 S.W. Griffith Drive
Beaverton, OR 97005
Phone: (800) 633-3676
(503) 643-1670

Medline Industries
1825 Shermer Road
Northbrook, IL 60062
Phone: (800) 323-5886

Miller & Sons Assoc., Inc.
New Rochelle, NY 10801

Owl Industries, Ltd.
177 Idema Road
Markham, Ontario L3R 1A9
Canada

Pfister Import-Export, Inc.
450 Barell Avenue
Carlstadt, NJ 07072
Phone: (201) 939-4606

Quinton Instruments
2121 Terry Avenue
Seattle, WA 98121
Phone: (800) 426-0538
        (206) 223-7373

Rasmussen, Webb & Company
First Floor
12116 Laystall Street
London ECIR-4UB, UK

Raven Equipment, Ltd.
Little Easton
Dunmow, Essex, CM6 2ES, UK

Ross Laboratories
625 Cleveland Avenue
Columbus, OH 43216

Rosscraft, Ltd.
14732 16-A Avenue
Surrey, B.C. V4A 5M7
Canada
Phone: (604) 531-5049

Salter International Measurement, Ltd.
George Street
West Bromwich, Staffs, UK

San Diego Blueprint
4696 Ruffner Road
San Diego, CA 92111
Phone: (619) 565-4696

Toledo Scale
431 Ohio Pike
Suite 302, Way Cross Office Park
Toledo, OH
Phone: (513) 528-2300

Index